The Holy Thief

The Holy Thief

A Con Man's Journey from Darkness to Light

Rabbi Mark Borovitz and Alan Eisenstock

WM

WILLIAM MORROW
An Imprint of HarperCollins*Publishers*

HarperCollins books may be purchased for educational, business, or sales promotional use. For information please write: Special Markets Department, HarperCollins Publishers Inc., 10 East 53rd Street, New York, NY 10022.

FIRST EDITION

Designed by Renato Stanisic

Printed on acid-free paper

Library of Congress Cataloging-in-Publication Data

Borovitz, Mark, 1951–
   The holy thief : a con man's journey from darkness to light / by Mark Borovitz & Alan Eisenstock—1st ed.
      p. cm.
   ISBN 0-06-056379-6
      1. Borovitz, Mark, 1951– 2. Rabbis—California—Los Angeles—Biography.
   3. Thieves—California—Los Angeles—Biography. I. Eisenstock, Alan.
   II. Title.

BM755.B623A3 2004
296'.092—dc22
[B]
                                                                    2004044905

04 05 06 07 08 WBC/RRD 10 9 8 7 6 5 4 3 2 1

*This book is dedicated to my wife/soul mate, Harriet,
my daughter, Heather, and all of the people who have
traveled the path of T'Shuvah/change with me.*

— M.B.

For the blessings in my house, Bobbie, Jonah, Kiva, and Z.

—A.E.

GOD IS MY ONLY FRIEND.
NO ONE ELSE KNOWS WHO I AM.
FIND A WAY OUT. FIND A WAY.

—Joseph Arthur, "Innocent World" from *Redemption's Son*

Contents

Introduction

I met this rabbi.

Picture the rabbi from central casting. Long white beard. Long black robe. Hunched over. Myopic. Soft-spoken. Inaccessible.

That's not him. Sixteen years ago Rabbi Mark Borovitz was in a prison cell. He was a mobster, gangster, con man, gambler, thief, and drunk. Then, trapped in a ten-by-ten-foot cage, he found his soul.

Before I met Rabbi Mark, I'd heard about people who were seeing him regularly. I was fascinated by this concept. There's an expression: "Everybody needs a rabbi." I had never been aware of anyone taking the expression literally. I wanted to find out more.

Rabbi Mark and I spoke on the phone and arranged to meet for coffee. We spent two hours that day talking. He was charismatic and forthcoming and I was intrigued. We started meeting once a week. I spent hours with him at Beit T'Shu-vah, "The House of Return." This is no ordinary synagogue. It is a combination house of worship and halfway house. Currently a hundred residents live there full-time, all battling addictions to drugs or alcohol. Many are people on the edge; some are dangerous to themselves and others. Rabbi Mark turns his back on none of them. Then, along with two hundred other worshippers, I attended services Friday night and on the High Holy Days. Rabbi Mark prowls the stage like a Jewish Van Morrison, shouting, singing, and wailing into his handheld microphone. These services *rock*.

I interviewed people Rabbi Mark counsels, and I sat in on their sessions. He meets *everyone*—all ages, backgrounds, lifestyles, and professions. You can be an adolescent or a senior citizen, a studio head or a crackhead. *No one is more important and no one is less important.* These are people seeking to control their addictions and learning to take control of their lives. Some are trying to pull themselves out of the black hole of despair; others are seeking merely to live life on a higher plane; some are looking for a lifeline; others are at the end of their ropes. He sees Jews, Christians, Muslims, Buddhists, agnostics, and atheists.

In other words, us. Rabbi Mark sees all of us.

This is his story.

—Alan Eisenstock

My Prayer

This book is my T'Shuvah. It is my Return.

For thirty years I lived a life of illusion. I was a magician of sorts. I specialized in cheap tricks, quick hits, and sleight of hand, especially when it came to writing checks. I got my audience's attention, then lured them into wanting to hand me their trust. I got them to believe in small miracles, if just for a moment, which was all I needed. And then I struck.

I know I cannot give everything back to everyone I have harmed. Even if I could, I know it would never be enough because I have stolen a part of people's souls. I know also that I cannot undo what I have done. I stand humbly here before you, any of you who have been my victims, and offer you a piece of my soul to take as your own.

In the end, there is no amount of money, no degree of apology, no amount of prayer that can repair the damage I have done to those souls. I can only attempt to repair my own soul, fill in the holes that have pierced my being, and return my refurbished soul into the world as evidence of the value and power of T'Shuvah, of repentance.

Forgive me, oh Lord, for I have sinned.

And sinned.

And sinned . . .

I am Redemption's Son.

The End

Tuesday, May 16, 2000.

A typical L.A. morning. Hazy brown sunshine, breeze-less, a chill in the air. The freeways are frantic. Shimmering four lanes of bumper cars.

I'm up, as usual, at 4:30 A.M.

Eyes slammed shut, I murmur my morning prayers. I shower, dress, hit my local Starbucks, swig back-to-back-to-back Rabbi Red-Eyes (one shot decaf, two shots decaf espresso), and flip through the paper at a table outside. I pop into the office by 5:15, surf through my e-mails, outline this week's Torah portion. At seven I strut into the sanctuary for my weekly men's Torah study. By eight I'm back in the office working the phones.

I argue with a D.A. in Kansas, plead with a judge in Kentucky, deal with a drug addict in North Hollywood. At eleven I return to the sanctuary to facilitate a weekly group on relationships. I break up the group at noon, graze through a chicken salad, settle into the conference room at twelve-thirty for our weekly staff meeting. By two, I'm at my desk banging more phone calls.

This day, at two-thirty, Harriet pokes her head in. She wears a charcoal-gray Donna Karan suit with subtle pinstripes and a smile that could light a night game.

"Mark," she says, "it's time."

She winks and goes. I grope under the mountain range of papers on my desk for my wallet. My intercom blinks. I pick up the phone. My secretary, Susan, announces that Lois, the mother of one of our residents, is on the line.

"Put her through," I say.

My chair groans as I lean back. I tuck a Stimudent into the corner of my mouth and click Solitaire onto my sleek flat computer monitor. I concentrate better when I doodle and Solitaire's my way of doodling.

Lois speaks slowly, solemnly. Her son has been living at Beit T'Shuvah for less than two weeks and is threatening to leave. If he does, he will violate his court order and will likely wind up in jail.

I don't see the kid bolting. He seems comfortable here, more so than in the parking structure where we found him, eating his dinner out of a garbage can. Amazing. This is a Beverly Hills family, entertainment business, big money. The dad produced a couple of movies you've seen, one of which was nominated for an Academy Award. Meanwhile their seventeen-year-old is popping uppers, drinking a six-pack of beer a day, financing his habit by hustling gay men on Hollywood Boulevard. One night the kid packed up and moved out of his six-thousand-square-foot mansion and into a doorway downtown.

"I'm so afraid he's going to leave," Lois says. "I don't know what to do."

"I know you're worried," I say. "I am, too."

"You are?" Her voice rises, veers toward panic.

"Yes." I scratch my forehead. "Lois, your son is an addict. With addicts there is only one thing you know absolutely and that is that you never know." I hold. "So I always worry. I'm always on my guard. And I don't feel that in your son's case, his main issue is leaving the facility. I think he feels secure here and that he wants to try. That's not to say we won't keep our eyes open. You know what I mean?"

Lois's breath whistles through the receiver. On my computer screen, all four aces line up at attention. I roll my mouse forward.

"Okay," Lois says. "Ok*ay*." Another rush of breath. "I feel better. I always feel better when I talk to you. Jesus, this is *hard*."

"You know it," I say. "And it's gonna get harder."

Lois swallows. "You don't mind if I call you when I get like this? When I get scared?"

"You *have* to call me. And I have to call you. Always. Constantly. Now that you have him back, you cannot let him go. So we'll be calling each other. And I will be talking to your son. Lois, he's here because he wants to be here. He wants to change."

"Thank you, Rabbi." A small laugh. "Not yet, right?"

"A few more hours. Then it's official."

"Well, early congratulations."

"Thank you. And Lois . . ."

"Yes?"

"Hang in there with him."

"I will."

"Remember," I say, "he is your son."

A click. Her throat? The phone? The line hums. I look up. Harriet appears in the doorway. She taps her watch. "Mark, we gotta go."

I stand, stretch, snag my coat from the hanger on the inside of my office door. I grin at Harriet like a game show host. "Yes, *dear.*"

I drive. I pull out of our parking lot, turn right onto Venice, and stop at a red light at Robertson. I drum my fingers on the steering wheel and lower my window. I crane my neck into the air and for the first time today, I allow myself a moment.

One moment. One memory. A memory of another moment fourteen years ago . . .

A *bus we called the Gray Goose, methodical, rickety, grinds up a back road to Chino State Prison, steaming into the barren brown horizon, the ground fluttering dreamlike outside the window.*

This is a bus of fools—silent, stoical, and severe men, men who have stolen, conned, or killed.

I am one.

The driver is a ghost. The silence cloaks all of us like a mist. I have taken this ride before, driven by other ghosts. Today, though, I know everything is different, everything has changed. I have been shaken into an otherworldly state of calm—of reverence—by a massive unseen force. A force that has spoken in a slow, deliberate Voice, delivering to me one simple and final truth: I will never take this ride again.

Because if I do, I will die.

*T*he light changes. I crawl forward into traffic. I breathe deeply and inhale the sounds of the street—the music of car engines, the rumble of the road, the rhythm of the horn honks. L.A. symphony. I shake my head.

"Amazing," I say.

"Finally hit you, huh?"

"Took me a while."

Harriet tips two cigarettes out of her pack and lights them both. She sticks one into my mouth. We exhale parallel lines of smoke.

"Hard to take it all in," I say.

"Given the history, it is pretty unlikely."

Unlikely. Perfect. Harriet has a way with words. She has the heart of a savior and the soul of a poet.

"Yeah," I say, "it's pretty fucking unlikely."

I glance at my wife. Consider her. My lover, my sparring partner, my reason, my heart, my soul mate. She feels my look on her. She reaches over to the steering wheel and covers my hand with hers. For a moment, we drive the car together.

"I couldn't have done it without you," I say.

Harriet smiles. "I know."

Inside Sinai Temple, in a room adjacent to the main sanctuary, my class gathers for dinner before the ceremony. There are twelve of us. We range in age from twenty-two to fifty-three. At forty-nine, I am the second oldest.

We eat nervously, quietly. After dessert we chant the Prayer of Thanks. As we finish and bow our heads in what will be our final prayer together, I become aware of a muffled hum on the other side of the wall: people gathering, talking, laughing. The noise builds, crests. I sip coffee, waiting for the nod to go in. Nobody moves. I head into the restroom.

In the bathroom, I stare at myself in the mirror. My nearly fifty-year-old face, full gray beard flecked with intermittent tinges of rust, stares back at me. The face is serene, the eyes watery. I am wearing a new camel-hair suit. I agonized over what to wear, rejecting several more conservative possibilities, including a jet-black suit that made me look like an undertaker.

I remove my gold-braided yarmulke. My bald head glistens with sweat. I grab a fistful of paper towels and pat my head dry. A classmate enters, a Jewish Abe Lincoln. His eyes cloud with concern. "You okay?"

"Superb," I say, my reflection smiling back at him. I replace my glasses and pivot away from the mirror, Abe at my heels.

In the dining room, we line up alphabetically. I am third. Rabbi Artson, the dean of the rabbinical school, looks us over as if inspecting his troops. He nods once, then we march single file out of the room.

The sanctuary is packed. People stand two deep against the back wall. Latecomers clog the doorways and cluster in the hallway. The sanctuary holds a thousand people. We're way past that; twelve hundred, I'm told later.

The organist slides into a chord. Our cue. We begin our walk down the center aisle toward our seats in the front row. I step dreamlike onto the plush maroon carpet. It feels as if I'm floating, and as I inch slowly forward, my hands begin to tremble.

And then, incredibly, the audience applauds. Tentatively at first, then with more confidence, more enthusiasm, then with outright joy. The audience stands, twelve hundred people as one, clapping, cheering, and a tidal wave of emotion sweeps through the room, catching me up, yanking me away, and then time freezes and I'm lost in a sea of speeches, prayers, songs, and teachings for more than two hours until someone calls my name and snaps me out of my trance.

I glance up from my seat. My sponsor, Rabbi Ed Feinstein, the rabbi who will present me to the Jewish community, the man who will explain in five minutes or less why I, Mark Borovitz, should, from this day on, be known as Rabbi Mark Borovitz, grabs my elbow and steers me to my feet. We climb onto the *bimah* and face the twelve hundred people before us. Ed looks at me and grins. Ed is my mentor, my teacher, and my best friend. He lowers his forearm onto the podium in front of him and addresses the crowd.

"The Chasidic master Rabbi Levi Yitzhak of Berditchev, a sainted ancestor of Professor Heschel, tells the story of a thief who lived a long and notorious life. Upon his death, he was sentenced to a permanent stay in hell."

The audience laughs. Ed smiles at me. My mouth folds into a smile and my shoulders rumble. Ed continues.

"Awaiting arraignment in Satan's courtroom, he noticed that beneath Satan's table, under the feet of the accuser, was a huge bag stuffed with Israel's sins, collected over the generations, that was made ready for Israel's foul condemnation before the heavenly judge. The thief realizes that it was for this moment that he was created. Deftly, with practiced dexterity, he lifts the bag and casts it deep into the fires of hell, saving Israel from eternal destruction. Distraught that his evil plan is foiled, Satan reaches to crush the soul of the thief. Suddenly, a heavenly messenger arrives and carries the thief into God's joyful presence. Rabbi Artson, the holy thief of Berditchev had very few descendants. It is my joy to present one."

I lose it. And so does everyone in the audience. They roar, and then they cheer, then applaud. I begin to laugh and then I start to cry. Standing next to me, Ed flicks a tear from his own cheek and keeps going.

"It is my joy," Ed repeats, "to present one as a candidate for ordination. For there are hundreds and hundreds of souls in our community that Mark has stolen back from death into life, from addiction into freedom, from darkness into light. As rabbis, we place at his hands our most powerful resource against death, against Satan's accusation. His is the work of a living Torah. Rabbi Artson, I present the Holy Thief of Beit T'Shuvah—Mark Borovitz."

Ed throws his arms around me in a bear hug, and then we kiss each other on each cheek, our lips splashing in the puddles of our tears. In my periphery, I see Harriet and my mother standing and crying, my brother Neal, also a rabbi, circling his arms around my mother, my daughter, Heather, next to him, sobbing. I am whisked off the stage, carried away as if on a wave, the voices, the laughter, the applause pulsating around me, echoing. I see Rabbi Jacob Pressman, distinguished, slightly hunched, one of the most respected rabbis in the city, shaking his head, as he, a consummate storyteller, grabs the microphone, his rabbinical candidate, the Jewish Abe Lincoln, standing at his elbow, blinking in confusion.

"They didn't tell me I was following Ed Feinstein," Rabbi Pressman says. "One thing I've learned over the years. Never follow a dog act or Ed Feinstein."

The room explodes in laughter. A hand massages my back. Harriet's? Ed's? I can't tell. I take off my glasses and dab my eyes with a camel-hair sleeve.

And then I get it. Through the water welling in my eyes, I absorb it all—this place, this time, these people, these symbols: the Torah, the candles, the *kiddish* cup, the yarmulke, the prayer shawl, the music, the language, and the Eternal Light—and I know that I have finally come home.

2

Home

MILLIE

She is a small, elegant, and pretty woman in her seventies. Her white hair is cut short and stylishly coifed. She is fond of family photos and distant memories.

Millie Borovitz sits tucked into the corner of her couch, clutching the arm for support. When she speaks about Mark, the youngest of her three sons and her second-youngest child, her lips pucker. Her voice is quiet and slow, her lips pursed, as though the words sting.

"I didn't know what he was doing," she says in a cracked, shadowy voice. "I didn't know. When I hear him tell some of the stories, I . . . I just can't believe he did those things. I blamed myself. What did I do wrong? Maybe I put too much responsibility on him. I don't know. I will never figure out what happened to him. Why he did all the things he did. I guess I'll never know."

Millie looks down, stares for a moment into her lap. She shakes her head, a tiny movement, over and over, again and again. She doesn't cry. She can't. In a lifetime of loss, her tears have all been used up.

The first time I got picked up by the cops I was three years old.

We were living upstairs in a duplex, right behind Lakeview Cemetery, where President James Garfield was buried, in a section of Cleveland called Coventry. One Sunday my father was out and my mother was taking a nap. My brothers were supposed to be watching me. My brother Stuart was nine and my brother Neal was six. They weren't paying any attention to me, wouldn't play with me. I was too young for them and I didn't talk much. I had a speech impediment; I couldn't pronounce my *R*s or *L*s. I was bored, so I decided to take a walk.

I made my way downstairs and went outside. It was a nice day, sunny. A soft breeze tickled my cheeks. I was a chubby butterball of a kid, with a mop of big red hair. Pretty hard to miss.

Nothing was doing on my street so I toddled down to the corner. Since I wasn't allowed to cross the street, I made sure to stay on my block. I turned left and kept going. And *kept* going. I didn't realize that I'd walked right out of Coventry into East Cleveland. Suddenly, a car rolled up next to me. A voice said, "Are you lost?"

I looked over and found myself face-to-face with a cop.

About this time my father came home and saw that I wasn't with my brothers.

"Where's Mark?" he asked.

They had no clue. They looked all over the house. Panicked, my father woke up my mother. "Mark's gone!"

My mother flew down the stairs and ran up and down the street, screaming my name. Meanwhile, my father called every police station in greater Cleveland. Finally, he phoned the East

Cleveland police station. "Do you have a little boy there named Mark Borovitz?"

I was sitting right there on the counter, eating an ice cream cone.

"Got a kid here," the cop said. "That's not his name, though."

"Red hair? Chubby?"

"Sounds like him," the cop said. "This kid says his name is Mock Butts."

"That's him!" my father said. "That's my boy!"

That story says it all. I was my father's boy and when he wasn't around, I got into trouble.

When I was five, my father bought our house at 3320 Beachwood Street. The neighborhood was close to everything, walking distance to all the schools, the park, and the synagogue. The house was perfect. We had an upstairs, a downstairs, a wide living room, a cozy dining room, full basement, a porch where we'd hang out on summer evenings, and a basketball hoop in the driveway.

We never locked the door. It wouldn't have mattered if we did since everybody knew that we kept the key in the mailbox. The house was always full, jammed with people. Every weekend was like one big party, people coming and going nonstop—aunts, uncles, cousins, friends, and kids from the neighborhood. The women would arrive in shifts, their arms loaded with platters of food. We kicked off the weekend with a bunch of us kids walking to shul Saturday morning, which I loved, and closed out Sunday night with a group of us playing cards around our kitchen table, which I also loved.

Having family around all the time goes back a generation. My grandparents had no children of their own. In the mid-1920s, right before the Depression, they adopted Jerry, my father. This small family quickly multiplied. My grand-mother had two sisters who married two brothers. Both of the sisters died in childbirth, after they'd already given birth to other children. My grandparents took in all of these children. They never told my father he was adopted and I don't think he ever knew. He grew up believing that his cousins were his brothers and sisters.

My father grew up with this whole clan of kids crammed into a tiny two-bedroom house. There were six of them—my father, Fayge, Nettie, Marty, Big Saul, and Little Saul, another cousin whom my grandparents took in. The kids were spread out all over that little house. One of the bedrooms had two three-quarter-sized beds. The two Sauls slept in one of the beds, the two sisters, Nettie and Fayge, slept in the other one. Marty slept in the bedroom with my grandparents, and my father slept on the couch in the living room.

Growing up, I was mesmerized by my uncle Marty. He was a hustler, a troublemaker. He had a stone-cold look to him, kind of like a Jewish Steve McQueen. He was dashing and dangerous. Rumors followed him everywhere. He was on the run, he was wanted, he was connected, he'd killed a man. He never denied any of it and I believed all of it.

I knew he carried a gun. He showed it to me once. I was ten. We were playing gin rummy and he had just beaten me, knocking with a two and taking me out. I was a king away from a fat gin that would've blown him away. He got to me first. Pissed me off. At our house, we took our cards seriously.

I needed some air. I shot out of the kitchen and bolted outside. It was late September, ten o'clock at night, and the cold was coming in. In Cleveland, the night chill rakes your face.

I sat down on our stoop. The screen door whipped open

behind me and someone stepped out. I knew it was Uncle Marty. I didn't even have to look up; I could smell his cologne. It was the good stuff, imported from Europe, he said. It smelled like money.

"Bad hit there, that hand," Uncle Marty said. "You're down now, what, five bucks?"

"I got careless," I mumbled.

"A little," he said. "Learned your lesson, I bet. Don't save pictures."

"I got greedy."

He shrugged. "You get greedy, you get burned."

I stood up. "Night's young. I'm gonna get you back."

Marty looked me in the eye. All he saw was steel determination. He pressed a crisp five into my palm.

"What's this?" I said.

"Your five. Call it school. Take it."

I pushed it back at him. "No way. You won it fair. Don't worry. I'll win it back."

Marty grinned. He took the bill, slipped it into his shirt pocket. "You can try."

He stretched. Underneath his coat something pearl white sparkled in the moonlight. He quickly closed his coat. I swallowed and nodded in the direction of his armpit. "Is that—?"

He was caught. "Yeah. I'm not gonna lie to you. It's a gun. I carry it for protection, that's all. My line of work. You know."

"You ever . . . used it?"

"No," he said, way too fast. He turned to go back inside the house. I grabbed his coat.

"Can I see it?"

The night shadows covered his face. He hesitated, then turned slowly back to me, and when he did, he was smiling.

"Sure," he said. He reached inside his coat, hauled the gun

out of a shoulder holster inside his coat, and handed it to me with two hands, as if he were letting me hold his baby. I took the gun from him. The handle was ivory, the barrel shiny and compact. I was surprised at the weight.

"Heavy," I said.

"Yeah, well," Uncle Marty said.

"Is it loaded?"

"What, are you kidding me? You think I'd bring a loaded gun into my brother's house? Come on."

Then, as I allowed the weight of the handle to fall full into my palm, Uncle Marty snatched the gun away from me and slid it back inside his coat in one lightning-fast move. He slapped his coat shut before I could contemplate touching the trigger. Uncle Marty lit a cigarette with a gold lighter he produced from a side pocket. He twisted his mouth and blew out the smoke.

"So that's it," he said. "No big deal."

I nodded, not sure what I was supposed to do or say. Uncle Marty rolled his cigarette from one side of his mouth to the other with his tongue. He toed the ground with an impressively shined brogue.

"Sometimes you gotta make a point," he said, eyeing the ground.

"Sure," I said.

"That's all." And then Uncle Marty laid a hand across my shoulder. "Let's go inside. It's cold."

I was also crazy about my uncle Harry, who married Nettie, my father's sister. Harry was the sweetest, most decent man in the world. Ironically, he owned a series of bars and strip clubs. The bar he owned when I was growing up was on 105th Street, near St. Claire and Superior. Sometimes on Saturdays, when I was nine or ten, I'd go to shul in the morning, then catch the bus over to Harry's bar. I'd spend the afternoon there helping out, sweeping the floor, washing glasses, and soaking up the atmosphere.

Harry was a heavy man. He moved slowly, planting each foot carefully as if he were testing the ground. He came from the old country and not only did he struggle with English, he also had a problem with his *R*s and *L*s, same as I did. I saw a lot of myself in Uncle Harry.

Uncle Harry was here semi-illegally. In the early 1930s, he jumped aboard a ship sailing from Hungary to join his brothers Louie and Jack. Within a couple of months, Harry opened his first bar, the Hot Spot, which featured, I'm told, stiff drinks and tepid burlesque. At the time, Elliot Ness was the police commissioner. A short mousy man with a pencil-thin mustache, Ness had it in for Uncle Harry. He made frequent unannounced visits to the Hot Spot, looking for any excuse to close Uncle Harry down.

One day, Uncle Harry opened his mail and pulled out a letter from the U.S. Army. It was his draft notice. Harry offered the government a deal. He'd go to war, if they made him a citizen. They went for it. So Uncle Harry fought in World War II and became a citizen at the same time.

Harry was a study in contradictions. My favorite was that even though he owned all these bars, he didn't really drink. He'd have an occasional schnapps Friday night to start *Shabbos,* and he might nurse a shot of booze on Sunday night at the card game. That one shot would last him all night. My father and Uncle Marty would kid him about it. Uncle Harry would kid right back.

"Hey," Uncle Harry would say, "I don't like to bring my work home with me."

I deeply loved my uncle Harry. And I loved hanging out at his bar. Customers would sit hunched over their barstools and pour out their life stories while Uncle Harry poured out their drinks. I began to notice similarities between bars and synagogues. They were both comfort zones, welcoming places where people, usually men, would gather every day to gossip, to complain, to ask for help and advice, to confess their sins, and to seek solace among close friends and occasional strangers. To me, they were both holy places.

MILLIE

The photographs lie all around her, in loose piles on the couch and in albums stacked on the coffee table. Millie goes through them deliberately, nodding every once in a while in recognition or in memory. Her lips remain pursed.

She stops at one photo. She absently brushes her thumb over it, cleaning it from any debris. The picture is of a man in a military uniform. Millie looks at him for an achingly long time.

"I remember the first time I met your father. I went to a meeting with some of my friends. I think it was for a political organization. Your father was at the head table and he was speaking. I turned to my friends and I said, 'I'd like to go out with him.' Turns out one of my friends lived next door to his best friend. She fixed us up."

Millie brushes the photo again and this time speaks to it. "I knew right away he was the one. Knew the minute we started dating. Then within two or three months he went into the service. World War II. I was seventeen. A year and a half later, when he came home on furlough, we got married. Yep. Soon as we started dating, I knew. I knew right away."

My father had a *look*. He always wore a long black overcoat and a homburg hat. For most of the year, the weather in Cleveland is brutal—cold, grim, and dark. Overcoat weather. Except for the summers, which are as hot and sticky as a sauna. Didn't matter to my father. He still wore his coat.

He looked like a rabbi. It wasn't just his appearance. It was his presence, his manner. People always knew where he stood. He was honest and moral and passionate. I truly believe he was a holy man. He loved people, loved to be around them. It was mutual. You'd say the name Jerry Borovitz and people would light up with recognition and with respect.

My father had a gift for knowing what each of his kids needed. He knew to be gentle with my brother Neal, stern with my brother Stuart, tough and funny with me. He believed that we should learn to be independent, to know how to fend for ourselves. We all played sports, and he insisted that we wash our own uniforms. He taught us how to use the washing machine.

"Your mother does enough," he said. "She doesn't have to do that, too."

He made us clear the table after dinner and wash our own dishes. And he insisted that we learn how to cook.

My father preached about the value of work. "A day's pay for a day's work, that's all you can expect from life." That was his mantra. He worked hard. He struggled to support us and he worked *hard*.

He left most of the household decisions to my mother. One of the decisions my mother had to make was when I should start elementary school. My birthday is November 1 and that put me in an awkward spot. She could hold me back a year, which would make me the oldest kid in kindergarten. Or I could start kindergarten when I was only four, making me the youngest kid in the whole school. I was smart and articulate, even though I'd started talking late, so my mother decided to put me in school.

It was probably a mistake. First, I wasn't totally potty-trained. No big deal when you're at home. *Major* deal when you're at school and on your own. The whole world knows when you have an accident. You're supposed to have that under control. Well, I didn't, not always, and a lot of the kids didn't want anything to do with me.

I felt like an outcast. I was young and immature. I didn't get some of the stuff that was going on. I was the butt of jokes. I tried to be cute, tried to cut up in class. I got a few laughs, but didn't make any friends. As I moved through kindergarten, then early elementary, I found that I never really fit in. I was constantly playing catch-up, always trying to get kids to like me, always trying to find my place in the group.

I was also fat, which didn't help. Kids made fun of me, both to my face and behind my back. It hurt. I tried not to let my feelings show, tried to pretend that what they said didn't bother me, tried to make jokes back. It didn't help. The more fat jokes I heard, the more I retreated into food. The worse I felt, the more I ate.

I also had a famously fierce temper. One time in gym class, in third or fourth grade, some kid put me down. I'd been having a bad day and I just lost it. I went for him. I pushed him against the wall and started pounding him. My face turned as red as my hair. I wouldn't stop. I kept whaling on him, then I got him down and starting slamming his head into the wood floor. I had gotten myself into a totally zoned-out state; I wasn't really conscious of what I was doing. I could feel myself being pulled off the kid and shoved into a corner. A strange calm came over me. The other kids were looking at me as if I were an alien creature, a monster, someone they wanted no part of.

At first I didn't care. I'd had enough of their taunts and stupid jokes, and I was tired of trying to fit in with them. I'd made some friends with older kids, kids who weren't bothered by my size and who seemed more in tune with who I was. I started hanging out with them. I became their mascot. The kids in my grade? Fuck 'em.

That's how I felt at first. After a while, I started caring a little more. I was only nine or ten. It was tough having no friends in my grade. I wanted kids to like me, wanted them to stop making fun of me.

It was around this time that I started stealing. Nothing big. Stuff from the corner store. Baseball cards, candy, marbles. Once I overheard a kid say that he'd like to have one of those balsa wood gliders, the kind you put together and throw in the air. After school, I went into the drugstore on Cedar Road, ripped one off, and gave it to him the next day. He was thrilled. We hung out at recess. He even let me fly the plane a couple of times. It was great. After that, I started stealing change and dollar bills from my mother's purse and giving that away to kids. They liked the money even better.

I know I was trying to buy their friendship.

The thing is, it worked.

Kids became nicer to me. They began talking to me more,

laughing at my jokes. They stopped ragging on me for being fat. They invited me to their parties. Life was getting easier. Easier, not great.

There was a day in August 1960 that was great. That was the day my sister, Sheri, was born. What a miracle she was. She was curious and funny and full of energy. Every afternoon after school, I'd wheel her in her stroller around the neighborhood, show her off, then come home and feed her a bottle. My mother didn't even have to ask me. I loved taking care of my little sister. Loved hanging out with her.

The other thing I loved was going to Saturday morning services. To me, shul was my home away from home.

The synagogue itself spoke to my soul. The building took up a whole city block. It looked like something out of a movie or a dream. It was a castle, a fortress, a masterpiece in concrete. Huge stone tablets of the Ten Commandments were sculpted into its side, and a dome of gold rested atop the structure like a giant skullcap. As I walked with my friends up the dozens of steps toward the massive front doors, I would pause and stare at the synagogue itself and I would get filled up with awe. As I walked inside the sanctuary, I would feel engulfed in a kind of *power.*

Once I settled into services, I would get lost inside the cantor's voice. Saul Meisels. This guy could sing. He reminded me of a Jewish Sam Cooke. Just like Sam, Saul had a sweet honey tenor. And like Sam, Saul took his time. He was in no rush. He'd latch onto a note he liked, hit it, and stay there, drawing it out, dipping up, down, and all around it, using his endless breath to take it *home.*

Most of the kids my age hated this. It was bad enough being in shul. It was torture listening to the cantor hang on to a high note for what felt like a month.

I loved it. I had no idea what Saul was singing. I didn't understand the Hebrew. It was the *music.* The music rocked me. I'd close my eyes and get swept away. It was as if I'd fallen under a spell. Everyone else was itching to get out of there, to go to the movies or to the park to play some ball. Not me. I wanted Saul to go on, hold the note longer next time, break his own record, and never stop.

My father was fighting for his life. I didn't know it at the time. I've often wondered whether if I had known, I could have done something to help him.

When my father got out of the army, he was trim and fit. Soon after, he put on a lot of weight. He got caught up in the lifestyle of the day: gorging himself on rich, fatty foods, smoking three packs of cigarettes a day, and avoiding exercise. He was also under a lot of stress. He was a traveling salesman, selling shoes. His route took him on the road constantly. He struggled mightily to make ends meet. His mission was to provide enough money for all of his kids to go to college.

When I was six or seven, my father quit his job. He was tortured by the decision. He loved being on the road, interacting with people, and he loved selling. At the same time, he hated being away from his family. He was offered a proposition that he couldn't refuse. At least it seemed that way. He bought into a reconditioned barrel business. After the deal was signed and sealed, he discovered that the previous owner had neglected to disclose a debt that came with the business— $20,000 that was now my father's responsibility.

Right after he bought the business, my father had the first of a string of heart attacks. He would have a total of seven in seven years. He had his first one in 1959. Nobody knew it was a heart attack. One afternoon, he was driving one of the barrel trucks. Suddenly, a pain shot through him. He was blinded for a split second. He swerved and lost control of the truck. A car smashed into him. He pitched forward and broke the steering wheel with his chest. He was rushed to the hospital, treated for his injuries and what the doctors thought was an ulcer, and released. Four months later, he had the chest pain again. This time the doctors knew it wasn't an ulcer. They realized now that he had a serious heart condition.

He began going slowly downhill, having heart attack after heart attack, one a year. One winter day when I was walking home from school, I heard the scream of a siren. A lump rose in my throat. I broke into a run. I flew around the corner and saw an ambulance parked in our driveway. The back doors were open, spread wide as wings. My father was lying on a gurney under a thin red blanket, his eyes narrow slits, his face white as the snow at his feet. Two paramedics in yellow jump-suits, wearing gloves and earmuffs, carefully lowered my father down our front steps. My mother trailed the gurney, her breath punching the air in milky gray circles. She dabbed at her eyes with a balled-up handkerchief.

I ran to my father's side. His fingers gripped my hand. He seemed scared and surprisingly small. I started to cry. He squeezed my hand.

"Hey," he said.

I sniffled, wiped my nose with my sleeve. And then he smiled at me. In the middle of being slid into the back of the ambulance, he *smiled.*

"I'll be all right," he whispered. "Don't worry. Just a precaution, all this. I'm gonna be fine."

Of course, I believed him.

Because I wanted to.

No. I had to.

My father got weaker and weaker. He couldn't give the barrel business his usual energy and attention, and finally the business folded. He went back on the road, selling shoes. After he came back from a trip, I saw that he didn't have the usual bounce to his step, his normal blustery good cheer when he burst through the front door. He walked slower and his face appeared paler, thinner. At night, fatigued, he'd settle on the living room couch. Sometimes I'd find him camped there, asleep, a blanket covering him, an unread magazine opened on his lap, a burning cigarette resting on the lip of an ashtray piled high with ash. After his sixth heart attack, I'd overhear my father and mother arguing nightly behind closed doors about money or, I should say, the lack of it. My mother soon announced that she'd taken a job at a retail store, for, I would discover later, minimum wage.

My father never stopped working, right up until the end. He even made it a point to take me with him on the road. He wanted to use the time we spent together in the car to talk. There was an urgency to these conversations, as if my father needed to divest his philosophical and ethical estate to me, impart his knowledge, experiences, wisdom. I listened silently. After a while, my father's voice would soften from physical strain and emotional exhaustion. I would lean forward to hear, and I would hang on every word.

"Mark, you have a lot of talent," he said once. "Problem is, you get distracted. That'll be your struggle. Keep focused. Keep your eye on the ball. Or you're going to get lost."

I took in everything he said. I repeated his words over and

over in my mind, vowing to live my life by them, hating myself when, ultimately, I forgot them.

My father died on Wednesday, January 12, 1966. I had just
come home from confirmation class. I was washing up
for dinner. My mother had just pulled a pot roast out of the
oven to cool. She walked into the living room to tell my father that it was time to eat. He was lying motionless on the
couch. She thought he was sleeping. He coughed once,
turned lazily onto his side, and closed his eyes. And that was
it. Just like that.

My mother screamed. I raced into the living room. I stared
at my father and I knew he was dead. My mother started to
shake. I wanted to hold her, wanted her to hold me. She
couldn't. She was in a state of panic and of finality. I ran into
the kitchen, grabbed the phone, and dialed 911. Then I gently
led my sister out of her room and walked her over to a neigh-
bor's house. I ran back home and covered my father with his
blanket. I called the doctor and then I called my uncles and my
aunts. My mother started pacing. I went over to her. We clung
to each other. Moments later, the paramedics arrived. They
opened the front door, and cold air from outside blew into our
house and knifed through me. Someone shouted instructions
and then the doctor walked in, followed by two men from the
funeral home.

I heard a car pull up. I ran outside. My uncle Harry and
aunt Nettie had parked in the driveway. They got out of their
car and walked toward me.

I said, "Dad's dead."

Aunt Nettie tilted her head and starting blinking violently

as if something had flown into her eye. I didn't think she'd heard me so I said again, "Dad's dead, Aunt Nettie. Dad's dead."

She said, "No," then, "*No!*" and she started hitting me, slapping at me, first with her fists, then openhanded, wildly swinging at me, screaming, "NO! He's not dead! How can you say that? You're lying!" and she just kept hitting me.

My uncle Harry said, "Nettie, stop," and wrestled her into a bear hug and pinned her arms to her side. My aunt Nettie wailed and flailed her arms, until finally, insane with grief, she crumpled to the ground and hugged herself, hysterically babbling, "No no no no no no."

Somehow my uncle Harry lifted her up and held her and held me and got us into the kitchen. My aunt and my mother grabbed on to each other. Then my uncle found a bottle of whiskey in the cabinet and poured himself a water glass full. He swigged half of it in one gulp and turned to me and said, "I promise you, as long as I'm alive, you will lack for nothing."

I couldn't respond. In a daze, I roamed back toward the living room. The paramedics had gone. The doctor was sitting at the dining room table filling out my father's death certificate. Then the two men from the funeral home picked up my father's body, placed him onto a gurney, and removed him from our house, forever. I felt suddenly and completely alone, and for a moment, I couldn't breathe.

The funeral was Friday morning, January 14, at Miller-Deutsch Funeral Home, on Taylor Road. The sky that morning was dark as night. A snowstorm threatened. The air hung heavy, like a pall.

The funeral parlor overflowed with people. A line of mourners stretched out onto the sidewalk. To accommodate the people outside, the funeral director's son climbed up on the roof and set up loudspeakers so the people on the street could hear.

It was a long service. A half-dozen people spoke glowingly about my father, the rabbi from the Heights Temple gave the eulogy, and Cantor Saul Meisels sang the traditional *El Maley Rahamim* prayer, his honey tenor drenched in heartache.

Everyone cried. Except for me. I knew that my life had forever changed. I knew that at fourteen years old, I had to grow up instantly, I had to be a man, I had to be responsible. There was no room for tears.

I was beyond grief. I felt dizzy and out of balance. My whole life I had counted on having my father's weight behind me to catch me if I fell. He was my support, my rock, my protector. I felt now as though a piece of my soul had been cut out of me.

After the service at the funeral home, we drove in a caravan of cars to the cemetery and we buried my father. One by one my brothers, my mother, my uncles, my aunts, my cousins, and our close family friends walked up to the grave and tossed dirt onto his coffin. I waited until everyone had finished. I walked up to his grave and sprinkled a handful of dirt onto my father's casket and, fighting the lump of grief that was rising in my throat, I turned away and stood off to the side. I closed my eyes and I whispered a prayer and promise.

"Dad, I'll say Kaddish for you every day."

That was my promise.

"I'll make you proud of me."

That was my prayer.

During the week of shiva, our family got together with our attorney and our accountant to settle my father's estate. We had the meeting around our dining room table. The first thing I learned was that my father had purchased a million-dollar life insurance policy, which he'd dropped two years before because he couldn't afford to pay the premiums. The second thing I learned was that my father was in debt. The barrel company never recovered from the $20,000 balance that was outstanding when my father bought the business. The accountant calculated that my father still owed various people close to $15,000, debts that were now our responsibility.

The lawyer argued that because my father had died, we no longer owed the money. The accountant said, "Two years ago, when the business went belly-up, I told Jerry that bankruptcy laws were made for honest people like him."

My mother sighed. "What are we going to do? We owe the money. I've got a son in college. Another one's got a wedding coming up . . ."

The lawyer folded his hands.

"Well," he said, "you can still declare bankruptcy."

"No," I said.

Everyone turned to me. The lawyer fastened a condescending smile on his face that I guess he thought would intimidate me. I met his eyes.

"The most important thing to my father was his good name. He said he would never go bankrupt. We have to honor that. We have to pay off his debts."

My uncle Harry leaned across the table. "Mark, these men, they know what's best—"

I stuck my face an inch away from his. "What would my

father have done, Uncle Harry? Would my father have declared bankruptcy? Never. He never would have done that. We're not gonna do it either."

The lawyer's smile faded. The accountant drummed his pen on the tabletop. No one dared speak. Finally, my mother nodded at my uncle Harry. He looked at me, shook his head, turned toward the lawyer and the accountant.

"See if you can settle out the debts," Uncle Harry said. He stood up. The meeting was over.

The accountant and the lawyer contacted everyone we owed. We settled with each one of them.

After we paid everybody off, we put $10,000 aside so Neal and I could go to college. We took what was left over for the family.

There was nothing left over.

A short time after my father died, my grandfather gave up his business, a tailoring and dry cleaning shop near downtown. It was 1966 and the neighborhood was no longer safe. He had been held up twice within a week. He reluctantly agreed to close his doors, if we promised to return the clothes he still had in storage.

"I have to give those clothes back," my grandfather said. "They're not mine."

"Pa, forget about the clothes," Uncle Marty said.

"Marty, they go back. And I don't care if the people pay or not. It's the right thing to do."

The next weekend, Uncle Marty and I unloaded the clothes from the store and stuffed them into a station wagon my uncle borrowed. My uncle had written down a list of my grandfather's customers. As we drove to the first address,

I started getting a little nervous. The neighborhood was run-down and inhabited by people who looked desperate and dangerous. We passed by clusters of young men hanging out at street corners and in front of liquor stores. I'd catch them glaring at us, their eyes registering steely looks of rage.

"Here's the deal," Uncle Marty said as he scanned street signs, searching for the address. "We bring the clothes up to the door. We tell 'em they can have the clothes back, for a price. They have to pay *something*. Five bucks, two bucks. We negotiate."

"What happens if they don't have any money?"

"They're fucked. They don't get their clothes."

"Grampa said—"

"I don't care what Grampa said. We're doing it my way."

We turned down a street lined with tiny houses shaped like cardboard boxes. Uncle Marty pulled up to the smallest one. Several teenagers stood across the street on a brown pockmarked lawn dotted with plastic beach chairs.

"Found it," Uncle Marty said, consulting the list. "Wallace. Go ahead, I'll wait here."

"*Me*? Why do I have to go?"

"I don't like to talk to people, you know that."

"I'm not going out there."

"The fuck you're not. Get out of the car."

"No way."

Uncle Marty reached into his coat pocket and flashed the pearl handle of his gun. "Don't worry. I got your back."

I stared at the gun. "What if you start shooting? You could hit me."

He leaned across the seat and opened the passenger door. "Duck."

I climbed out of the station wagon and slouched to the

back. I flipped up the hatch and hauled out an armful of pants, shirts, sweaters, and dresses encased in plastic cocoons. Balancing the pile of clothes in my arms, I trudged to the front door.

I sneaked a fist out from beneath the clothes and knocked on the doorframe. A woman in a housedress appeared. She was stooped and frail and walked with a limp. The top of her head was wrapped in a colorful handkerchief. She reminded me of my grandmother.

"Yes?"

"I have your clothes," I said.

She cleared her throat and opened her mouth slightly, revealing a toothpick.

"My grandfather had them in his store," I said. "He's going out of business. I want to give them back to you."

The woman looked past me, into the street. She ran the toothpick over her bottom lip, then plucked it out of her mouth and allowed it to flutter to the floor. We both watched it fall. She placed her shoe over it, crushing it as if it were a cigarette butt.

"I can't take them."

Her voice sounded like a faraway echo. At first, I didn't understand.

"They're your clothes," I said. "They belong to you."

"I don't have any money to pay you."

I glanced back at Uncle Marty in the station wagon. He was coiled over the steering wheel. His left arm dangled outside the driver's window, a cigarette cupped in his palm. He tilted to his right and rolled down the passenger window, making sure, I imagined, that he had a clean shot. He tipped the brim of his hat, a gunslinger in his own private cowboy movie.

The woman stared at the floor. "Sorry."

"No, no, you shouldn't be sorry. Listen, anything, it doesn't matter. Do you have . . . a dollar?"

"Don't have a dollar. Don't have fifty cents."

And not wanting to face me anymore, not being able to endure what was surely unbearable humiliation in front of this fourteen-year-old collector who stood at her door, his arms laden with her family's clothes, clothes that I knew she needed, she turned to walk away.

"Here," I said pushing the screen door open with my shoulder. "Please. Take them."

"I told you, I don't have any money—"

"It's okay. Please. They're yours."

I shoved the pile of clothes at her. She hesitated, then looking somewhere beyond me, the woman limped back toward me. The plastic wrapping around her clothes crinkled as I laid the pile into her arms. She staggered for a second under the surprising weight, then disappeared into the darkness of her hallway. I removed my wallet, pulled out a dollar, and stuffed the bill into my shirt pocket. I rushed through the screen door and walked back to the car. I barely had time to close the door before Uncle Marty sped away like a getaway driver.

"What'd you get?"

"A dollar?"

"That's it? A dollar for all those clothes?"

"That's all she had."

Disgusted, Uncle Marty flicked his cigarette out his open window.

"Fuckin' deadbeat," he said.

And so it went for the rest of that afternoon and the following day. One by one, Uncle Marty and I drove to

every name on my grandfather's list. I was always the delivery-
man, lugging armfuls of clothes to each front door while
Uncle Marty, my backup, stayed in the car, enjoying a smoke.

Only a few people paid. I paid for the ones who couldn't—
a dollar, fifty cents, a quarter. By the end of the afternoon, I was
out of money. That night, while my mother slept, I pulled a
handful of dollar bills out of her purse to finance the rest of my
grandfather's customers.

Truth is, I kind of enjoyed the game. I liked making up
phony stories to tell my uncle, each one sadder or more colorful than the one before. Looking back, he probably knew I
was bullshitting him. Or maybe he thought I was a pathetic
bleeding heart. He'd never tell me. Every once in a while,
though, he'd throw me a curve.

"Fifty cents? That's all they gave you? That's ridiculous.
I'm going back there and shake them down."

I couldn't back off my story. I had to play it out. "Fine,"
I said, "see if you can do any better."

He paused, pretended he was about to turn the car around,
then thought better of it.

"Fuck it. Ain't worth my time."

There was another piece to all this. Something I couldn't
put my finger on. A feeling . . .

What I didn't know was that by returning the clothes and
paying for them with my own money, I was performing a
mitzvah. A good deed. An act of kindness. What I did know
was that the act itself was its own reward. I didn't do it for any
reason other than it felt right. When I finally gave back all the
clothes, I actually felt *uplifted*.

I wanted to share this feeling. With whom, though? I
couldn't share it with my uncle Marty, who sat in the front
seat of the station wagon with the engine idling and his finger

on the trigger. My brothers or my mother wouldn't understand. My sister was too young.

I would have been able to tell my father.

He was the one person who would have understood. And
he would have explained that what I had done was in fact a holy
act. He would have answered all of my questions and he would
have let me talk as long as I wanted and he would have listened.

Yes. I would have been able to tell my father.

3

The Beginning

SHERI

Sheri Borovitz-Linda speaks in a radio voice, confident, husky, and clear.

"After Dad died, Mom went to work. Every afternoon, Mark would pick me up from the babysitter. He was probably as responsible for me as my mother was. I would go everywhere with him. I used to tag along with him when he went to his synagogue youth group. I'd play cards with him and his friends. Oh, and I beat him. I was only seven years old. He pretended to be upset. I think he was secretly proud of me. His little sister, the card shark."

She laughs. "I remember once he was supposed to take me to the movies. Instead we went bowling with a bunch of his friends. I was eight, he was seventeen. He wasn't watching me and I fell over the bowling ball and cracked a tooth. He freaked out. He was afraid my mother would kill him. He was always doing stuff like that. Running me around with him to places I shouldn't have gone. You know what? I loved it."

Sheri speaks now through a tiny catch in her throat.

"When I had appendicitis, he's the one who took me to the hospital. I was in excruciating pain. My mother was at work; we

couldn't get to her. Mark took me to two doctors, then rushed me to the hospital. I was lying on a gurney, writhing. He was just about to forge my mother's name to admit me into surgery when she came out of the elevator. That was Mark. He'll find a way. God, we did so much together . . ."

Financially, we were drowning. My mother would bring home her paycheck and she'd agonize over whom to pay and whom to put off. Then, out of the blue, a friend offered her a job working in accounts receivable for a housewares distributor. It was an opportunity to begin a career. She grabbed it.

The money was still not enough. The bills mounted up. I could see the strain on my mother's face. She was sleeping less, working more, and worrying constantly.

I couldn't stand seeing her this way. It was breaking my heart. I knew there was only one way out. I decided to take it.

I went to see Mario, the barber.

Mario had given me my first haircut when I was four years old. The day is etched in my memory. I sat atop two Cleveland phone books in the barber chair, screaming my lungs out while Mario snipped away and my mother circled around me snapping pictures with the new Kodak camera she'd bought for the occasion. After a few minutes, my crying slowed, calmed by Mario's soothing singsong voice: "Looking sharp, Markie boy, looking *sharp*." He tantalized me with a bribe, offering me a Tootsie Roll pop and a stick of gum if I'd stop wailing. That closed the deal. I stopped crying. Hey, I was four. I was easy.

Mario's barbershop was tucked into a quartet of storefronts on Lee Road, right off the corner from one of the main streets in Shaker Heights. Mario's looked just like the barbershop you'd see in a 1950s photograph in *Look* magazine—a broad glass front window wide as a movie screen with an old-fashioned barber pole rotating beside it. Pure Norman Rockwell.

Mario was short, taut, trim as a dancer, and just as quick on his feet. He moved in short, sharp box steps, back to front, jabbing lightning fast with his scissors. He had a full head of black hair combed back like Sinatra's. He wore a dark pencil mustache and smoked an Italian rope cigar. Mario smiled constantly, a thin, crafty smile that hinted he knew more than he'd ever tell. Everything Mario did was fast. He talked fast, worked fast, moved fast, laughed fast. Thin as he was, Mario was not someone you'd want to mess with. There were rumors. He was once a button man for the Cleveland mob. He had a list of hits in the double figures next to his name. He was a professional entertainer, a singer and comedian, and he'd had his own radio show.

What was true was that Mario was a fence, and Mario's barbershop was a mob front.

Everybody knew it. You could tell by Mario's clientele, Italian men in suits, businessmen arriving without appointments for a shave and a haircut. These men had priority. If I was in the middle of a haircut and one of the Boys walked in, Mario would whisk the smock off me and ask me to wait. He'd finish me up later. Right now, he had to give Mr. Tony Damiano a trim and a singe. I would scramble out of the barber chair, brush the seat clean of any loose hair, and move off to the side as Mr. Damiano sat down in my place. He'd nod at me and wave his pinkie in appreciation. I'd nod back and sit patiently while Mario would singe the ends of Mr. Damiano's hair with a match, the Sicilian way to keep the hair even and devoid of any loose or dead strands. Mario was old-school.

While I waited, I breathed in the thick air in the barbershop, which smelled of cigar smoke and aftershave, and I'd overhear heated conversations beneath hot towels, bargains struck across barber chairs, deals brokered, bets made and collected, conflicts resolved, pleas heeded and refused. Sometimes a man who came in to Mario's for a shave and a haircut Saturday afternoon would appear in the newspaper obituaries Monday morning. The following week, if a man returned for a haircut after a heated argument with Mr. Damiano, I would catch Mario's eye. Mario would wink back and after the man left, Mario would say through his omnipresent white smile, "That guy? Tommy Barolo? Had a close shave."

My mother had known Mario for years. He had once dated one of her cousins. They had gone out for months, had gotten pretty serious, then broken up because of religious differences. Mario never had any hard feelings.

From the time I was eight or nine, my mother would drop me off at Mario's Saturday afternoons while she ran errands. When I got older, I took the bus to Shaker Heights myself and I would hang out for the afternoon. I would help out, sweeping up hair, folding towels, shining shoes, washing the front window, hosing down the sidewalk. I became The Kid, the mascot, Mario's sidekick, and eventually, I became Tony Damiano's adopted godson.

One afternoon, right after the start of tenth grade, while my mother was at work and my sister was in day care, I took the bus from school and went to see Mario. The bell above the door jangled as I walked in. Mario was soaking his combs in alcohol. In the corner of the shop, the black-and-white Sylvania was tuned to the Indians' game.

"Come on, ya bum," Mario said to the TV, "learn how to *bunt*."

I stuffed my hands into my pockets, studied my shoes. Mario tilted his head toward me. He saw right away that something was up. "You all right?"

"I need to talk to you, Mario."

"What's the matter?"

I took a deep breath. "I've got to help Mom."

"She sick?"

"No." Then I just blurted it out. "We need money."

Mario patted his lacquered black hairdo to make sure it was still in place. He walked to the front door and flipped over the "Open" sign. The other side read: "Taking Five."

Mario rested his hand on my shoulder and squeezed. "Come with me."

He spun on his heel and, walking in crisp, staccato steps as if he were tap dancing, headed into the basement. I followed him down the stairs. He hit a light switch. I blinked. We were standing in a bachelor pad right out of *Playboy* magazine. I took a step and my feet plunged into ankle-deep, purple shag carpeting. A leather couch, which allegedly opened into a king-size bed, filled most of the room. A mahogany bar, liquor bottles lined up on top in rows like soldiers, glistened against the far wall. Next to the bar, on a bookcase crammed with LPs, a record player sat between twin speakers. A Lava lamp teetered on a teak end table.

Mario shot through the room. I followed, nearly clipping his heels. He stopped at a second door and yanked a key ring out of his pants pocket. He jingled a dozen keys, located the one he wanted, and opened the door. Mario flicked a wall switch and a bank of florescent lights popped on, bathing the room in stark white light, bright as an operating room.

Tiered shelves, floor to ceiling, circled the room, straining under the weight of merchandise: stereo equipment, radios, tape recorders, toasters, waffle irons, mixers, coffeemakers, portable grills, records, jewelry, shirts, pants, sweaters, shoes, pots, pans, dishes, and flatware. A small city of color television sets crammed into cardboard boxes loomed in the center of the room.

Everything, of course, was stolen.

"It's like a department store," I said.

"We got it all," said Mario. "And if you don't see it, don't worry. We got it. It's just not on display."

"On display," I repeated.

"So . . . you need money?"

I kicked at an imaginary object on the cement floor. "Yeah. See, Mario, my mom's job isn't—"

Mario held out his palm like a stop sign. "First rule. Your business is your business. Nobody has to know anything. Okay?"

I nodded.

"Here's the arrangement. Sixty-forty to start. Things go good we can renegotiate. Everything you see in here's for sale. Even better, it's on consignment. You know what that means, right?"

"No," I said.

"It means you're not stuck with it. You can take something out of here and try to sell it and if you can't move it, bring it back. And remember: If your customers want something and you don't think you got it? You're wrong. We got it. Whatever they want, we got. *Capisce*?"

"Yes."

Mario placed a gentle arm around my shoulder. I was fourteen years old and we were almost the same height.

"Welcome to the business, Mark," he said.

I started with watches. Cool, space age, and multifunctional. They contained both a stopwatch *and* alarm clock, featured a flexible and durable band, and were available in three attractive colors. I brought a box to school. I wore one to homeroom, flashed it around, set off the alarm.

I was deluged at my locker: half the football team, most of the student council, the drama club, the chess club, some of the school orchestra, even a couple of cheerleaders. I was sold out by noon.

Next I got into jewelry—rings, necklaces, and bracelets, then T-shirts, sweaters, records, and radios. I started lugging stuff out of Mario's basement and loading up my locker. I never kept any books in there so I had plenty of room. I quickly learned the basic rule of economics: supply and demand. In my case, the demand was way bigger than my supply. I found two empty lockers and filled them up with inventory. I now had three lockers containing everything except a book. Kids began branching out, asking for concert tickets, easy gets like Tommy James and the Shondells or Neil Diamond, then impossible sold-out tickets to the Beatles or the Beach Boys, which took a day or two. The money poured in. Before I knew it, I was making four hundred dollars a week, cash, and Mario upped me to a full partner.

I gave a lot of it to my mother. I'd shove a stack of bills into an envelope and slip it into her purse. I told her I'd gotten a part-time job. This was true. I had started working weekends at a record store in downtown Cleveland called

Record Rendezvous. If my mother was suspicious about the amount of money I was bringing in, she never let on.

I also gave money to my brother Stuart, who had started gambling and losing. Poor Stuart had begun a lifetime of chasing the sure thing and always coming up short. I couldn't stand to see him in debt. I sent him money for rent and clothes, sometimes as much as $500 a month. Whatever he needed, I gave him.

And I gave money away to my friends. Well, kids I was trying to acquire as friends. I would buy them gifts in hopes that they would include me in their group. It worked. They hung out with me at school and invited me to their parties.

I knew that they weren't real friends. I knew they were using me. That didn't stop me. I kept buying them presents and giving them cash.

Because having fake, superficial friendships was better than having no friendships at all.

The year my father died, I went to temple every day and said Kaddish for him. I'd chant the prayer standing next to old men who spoke broken English or no English at all, the same men every day. I had nothing in common with these men and yet I felt that I fit in with them. It was probably because I felt no pressure to impress them.

The men and I formed a sort of family. When I would stand and say Kaddish for my father, I wasn't alone. They were all standing and saying Kaddish, too. We were praying and remembering together. We were all part of the same club, a club that had only one requirement for membership: You had to have lost a loved one. As we prayed, we nodded silently to one another. We knew; we understood.

In this life, the synagogue life, I was the epitome of the Good Jewish Boy. I certainly looked the part. I was heavyset and wore glasses and looked studious, although I hardly ever cracked open a book. I was polite and helpful. I'd help the Sisterhood set up for brunch and after services I'd put away the prayer books and prayer shawls. I became active in our temple's chapter of United Synagogue Youth, a national Jewish teen organization. We held meetings, sponsored fund-raisers and dances, involved ourselves in Jewish social action. In a couple of years, I became chapter president.

That year, though, I was the object of the community's perpetual sorrow. I received countless well-wishes, innumerable words of advice, infinite recollections of my father's wonderfulness.

It was too much. I thought I would explode from the sincerity of the congregation's good wishes. They wanted so much to be there for me, unaware that the only thing I wanted was to have my father back.

I would escape into the chapel with my "family." I would lumber down the aisle and hide out in the front row. Invisible in plain sight. I would fold my hands, stare at the Eternal Light, wait for Kaddish, and lose myself in the company of old men. Every day the year my father died.

The first bar I hung out at was the King's Pub on Cedar Road. It was quiet and friendly, a kind of cave in dark wood paneling. A jukebox played jazz—Louis Armstrong, Ella Fitzgerald, Miles Davis, Stan Getz. Cigarette smoke snaked up to the ceiling. The air reeked of draft beer and English Leather.

Inside the King's Pub, time and place evaporated. I would

take a seat at the bar or at a table snug against the wall and I could be anywhere. I felt transported to some other location, a different city even, somewhere far from Cleveland, far away from my life. I looked a lot older than I was—fifteen—and John, the bartender, never carded me. In the Pub, nobody gushed over me with sympathy, nobody asked me any questions, nobody tried to fix my life. I was just another guy in a bar.

I became a regular. The location was perfect—equidistant from my house, the high school, and the Heights Temple. I started leaving the phone number of the Pub for business purposes. If Mario or a customer needed to get in touch with me, they'd call me at the King's Pub and leave a message with John. The Pub was my place. I loved the smell of greasy burgers crackling on the grill and the sound track of glasses clinking and people laughing without fear.

My life was a twisted, crazy dance, going in a thousand directions at once. I'd wake up, go to school, cut most of my classes, sell shit out of my lockers, go to temple, run the USY meetings, say Kaddish, and drink at the King's Pub. I also worked at Record Rendezvous, took care of my sister, and helped around the house.

Mainly, I schemed to make more money. If someone at the Pub came up with a plan that seemed hot, I'd run it by Mario, see if he wanted a piece. If he did, I'd grab a little taste for myself, Mario and the Boys would take their cut, and I was a hero. If Mario didn't like what he heard, he'd pass and I'd go all in. Sometimes the deal was a slam dunk and sometimes I'd get burned. Didn't matter. Making the big score was always what drove my engine.

As I began senior year, my mother started pressuring me about college. I honestly didn't want to go. It seemed like a waste of time and money. I already had my career path laid out. I was going to be a hustler. What could college teach me about that? Business was going well. I was making five hundred bucks a week . . . and I was in *high school*.

My mother wouldn't let go.

"You're too smart not to go to college," she said.

I just smiled and shrugged, which drove her crazy. She wasn't winning this argument with me. I didn't see the point of college. Exasperated, my mother pulled out her ace in the hole.

"You're going to college," she said, "because you promised your father."

She won.

I don't remember filling out the application. Maybe my mother did it herself or maybe I did it one night when I was drunk. In any case, some time around February, there was a fat envelope waiting for me when I got home from school. I had been accepted at Ohio State.

The year I started Ohio State, 1969, the country was in turmoil. The Vietnam War was in full swing, and student demonstrators blanketed the campus daily. I was staunchly antiwar and would have joined the protests if only I'd had the time.

I was too busy being a gangster.

One thing I knew about college students—hippies, straights, jocks, nerds, antiwar protesters, or ROTC Republicans—they all loved to drink. And when people drink, they often enjoy making a bet. I married these two ideas and turned my dorm room into a casino.

I had some help from my roommate. When I first saw

Sean, I thought we'd have nothing in common. He was a tall, soft-spoken Catholic who always carried a briefcase. As soon as I met him, I was trying to figure out how to get rid of him.

That was until he opened the briefcase. Inside he kept bottles of VO, scotch, and vodka, Bloody Mary mix, a jigger, a strainer, a row of shot glasses, and a clump of swizzle sticks. His briefcase was a mobile minibar. Unlike me, Sean would go to all the protests. He'd hang out in the Quad, listen to the speeches and the antiwar songs, and try to pick up girls. Meantime, I was back in the dorm room running a blackjack game and sports book. Business was booming. After a long, hard day demonstrating, there's no better way to unwind than chugging a couple of tall boys and gambling on your favorite team.

By the spring of 1970, I'd had it with college. I'd only enrolled because I promised my mother I'd give it a try. Well, I tried it. Didn't like it. College was slowing me down, getting in my way. I wasn't learning anything. I wanted to know how to become a millionaire before I turned twenty-five, legally or illegally, it didn't matter. For some reason, Ohio State didn't offer that course. So fuck it. I dropped out.

In 1970, I began a seven-year stretch of hustling, drinking, and madness that plunged me into perpetual darkness. I saw nothing except the night.

Work was my anchor. I always needed a legitimate job, something that gave me structure and a steady paycheck and made me feel human. The job, though, was never enough. The job was a symbol that I had tumbled into the status quo, that I was on a path to becoming just another blue-collar working stiff. I could not abide that. I craved the rush of action and the promise of riches. So I schemed, conned, and scammed, planning an escape route from this life into another life, a far more glamorous life. My plans were vague, often crooked, usually cooked up when I was shitfaced. I enlisted a series of partners, all of them like me, dreamers, schemers, lowlifes, and drunks. We planned our futures in bars on the backs of cocktail napkins. By the end of the night, our fortunes depended on retrieving the near-illegible scribbles smeared into oblivion by splashes of liquor and streaks of lipstick. We became millionaires in our minds. We giddily imagined truckloads of cash rolling up to our doors. One surefire swindle involved luring unsuspecting senior citizens into buying condominiums in Florida that had been thrown together in three weeks and embedded in swampland. This venture blew up after we invested our own money in brochures. A real estate company found us out and blew the whistle. We retreated into a series of quick hits, the most elaborate of which was selling car telephones to drug dealers.

We called ourselves "rounders." We made the rounds of the local bars—the King's Pub, the Proud Pony, the Virginian, the Brown Derby, the Bluegrass. I would get off work at five, head immediately to one of my bars, eat dinner, drink until the bar closed, then go to an after-hours joint and drink some more. At two or three in the morning, I'd stagger to my car and drive home, sleep off the long night, and get up and out the door at 9 A.M. for work.

Some nights I'd pick up a girl, a rounder like I was. I'd ply her with manhattans and quaaludes I'd bought from a doctor I knew. We'd go to her place or use the living room couch at a friend's or the back bedroom at my cousin's. It was cheap and sleazy and I was drunk and stoned and anaesthetized and worst of all, I didn't care. The next evening I'd go to a different bar, pick up a different girl, and have the same fucking night. Nothing made sense; nothing felt right. I longed to meet a decent girl, a near impossibility since I spent every waking moment in the same bars, with the same people, doing the same shit.

Each one of those bars was my office. My desk was a back table. From there I sold Mario's hot merchandise and ran countless scams. My pockets bulged with cash, cash I somehow managed to spend faster than I earned. I'd give money to my mother, my brother, and to people whom I wanted as friends. I'd overtip the bartenders and the waitresses. I'd buy everybody in the bar another round and treat my table to dinner. I'd run a tab at five or six different bars at the same time. My bar bills swelled to three thousand dollars a month.

Through it all, I continued to go to temple. I'd attend morning services, make the minyan, and sometimes stop at shul after work before settling in for the night at the King's Pub or the Virginian. Then, the more I drank and the more I hung out at bars, the less I went to temple. When I did go, I recognized fewer people. The crowd seemed younger. The old guys, my minyan men, hung out by themselves, respected and ignored.

The year after I left Ohio State, I decided to say Kaddish for my father on Yom Kippur. I was broke. I had gone through my usual monthly crash and burn: started strong, raked in a ton of cash, spent it, gave it away, earned another windfall through some dubious hustle, built my stake back up, then promptly lost that, too. I couldn't account for where the money went. It flew out of my hands as if blown by a wind.

My mother couldn't afford to buy tickets for the High

Holidays. It didn't matter to me. I just wanted to go to temple for an hour, say Kaddish, and leave.

The High Holidays were late that year. It was mid-October and Cleveland was experiencing an early freeze. A layer of frost covered my car. I started to scrape off my windshield, said screw it, and decided to walk to temple. It was a cloudy, overcast morning. The cold bit at my cheeks, and a few snow flurries dusted the top of my head. I had on a suit, no topcoat. I shivered and put up my collar.

I turned the corner to the Heights Temple. People decked out in expensive suits, dresses, and overcoats climbed up the concrete steps toward the sanctuary. I walked up the stairs slowly. A man I recognized, a friend of my father's, stepped in front of me. I smiled, extended my hand.

"*L'a shona tovah,*" I said, wishing him a good year.

He grinned shyly, as though my greeting made him uneasy. "*L'a shona tovah,*" he said. He moved his feet a shoulder's width apart.

"Looks like winter's come early," I said.

"Yes." He nodded enthusiastically, then in an urgent whisper said, "Mark, do you have a ticket?"

"Excuse me?"

"I can't let you in without a ticket."

"Look," I said. I stared at him, my eyes clouding over, appealing now for understanding. "Things are a little tough for our family right now. So, come on, we've been members for years. I just want to say Kaddish for my father."

I waited, thinking that was the end of it. I started to walk by. He slid to the side and blocked my path as if he was a bouncer. "I'm sorry."

I blinked at him, not comprehending. "It's Yom *Kippur*." I didn't know what else to say.

"I'm very sorry," he said. "You're going to have to go."

"Half an hour. Just to say Kaddish."

"I can't do it, Mark. I'm chairman of the membership committee—"

I glared at him, and then I spoke in a voice that came from a part of me I'd never known existed.

"What kind of Jew are you?" I snarled.

"If I let you in, then I have to let everyone in who didn't buy a ticket—"

"Fuck you."

"What did you say?"

"I said . . ." I put my mouth right next to his ear and I shouted at the top of my lungs, *"FUCK YOU!"*

I turned and fled down the stairs.

I did not set foot in a synagogue again for ten years.

When I was twenty, I started carrying a gun. Of course, you couldn't legally own a gun until you were twenty-one. That was okay. The gun wasn't registered anyway.

I got the gun one night in a bar. Didn't ask for it, didn't really want it. I just got it. My uncle Marty handed it to me. It looked exactly like the pearl-handled revolver he'd shown me ten years before.

"Here," he said, "take this."

"Why? I don't need it."

"Just take it. For peace of mind."

"I have plenty of peace of mind."

"My peace of mind," he said.

Uncle Marty pressed the gun into my hand and walked out of the bar. End of conversation.

I never used the gun. One time, though, I came close.

My sister was in the seventh grade. She was twelve and I was twenty-one. I stopped home after work one day and I found her curled up on the living room couch, crying her eyes out. I'd never seen her so upset.

"Sheri, what's the matter?"

"My best friend told me she can't see me anymore," she managed to choke out between sobs. I put my arms around her, rocked her gently. It took her a while to calm down.

"Why did she say that?"

Sheri blew her nose into some tissues I handed her. She hesitated before she spoke. I could see she was deciding if she should tell me. She crumpled up the tissues and lobbed them into the wastebasket.

"It's her father," Sheri said.

She shook her head, and her eyes started leaking again. She took a deep breath. "Her father told her that Daddy was no good and neither were you and she couldn't talk to me anymore."

I let the words float in the air. "That's what this guy said?"

"Words to that effect."

"I bet."

"The words don't matter, Mark. She was my best friend. *Was.*"

She started crying again. I held on to her, let her cry until she was cried out. I squeezed her, probably too hard, because inside I was livid. No, beyond livid. I was murderous.

"Sheri, let me tell you something. It's very important."

Her eyes were swollen and red from crying. She ripped a fistful of tissues out of the box and clenched them.

"Your father was a great man," I said. "He was revered. People loved him and looked up to him. Hundreds of people came to our house to pay their respects after he died. I'm serious. *Hundreds*. Look, I can't make this girl your friend. She will apologize to you tomorrow, though, I can promise you that."

I stood up.

"Sheri, your father was a great, great man. Never forget that."

I was out the door.

I knew the girl's father. His name was Stanley. He was a rounder, a two-bit hustler, and a wannabe. If we were in the same bar, I'd catch him staring jealously at our table, wishing that he could be sitting with us, maybe wishing he could trade places with me. Yeah, I knew this guy. He was lowlife piece of shit.

I knew where he lived. I waited an hour or so. I wanted to cool down. I hit the Pub and belted back a couple of strong ones. Thought that might put a little water on my fire. Funny thing. The liquor just torched me. My anger blew up inside me. My father had been dead for more than seven years and my feelings were as raw as if he'd died yesterday. I stood up at the bar, slammed back one more shot for the road, and patted my side just to be sure. Yep. I had my gun.

I was going to kill this motherfucker.

I went over to Stanley's house. I walked around to the back. It was late evening. Shadows were lying across his patchy lawn. I rapped on the door, hard and long.

"I hear you, I hear you, I'm coming."

I paced outside. It seemed like it took an hour for Stanley to make it to the door. He peered through his window, saw me, and screeched to a stop on the linoleum floor in his kitchen. He looked down at his feet. He wasn't wearing shoes.

"Hello, Stanley," I said.

"What do you want?"

"We need to talk."

"What about?"

"It's kind of sensitive. Personal. Better if we talked outside."

He paused. Considered whether he should open the door. "I'm not wearing shoes," he said.

I smiled. "It'll just take a second, Stan."

He still hesitated. Then he realized he couldn't back down. He knew he had to come out and deal with me face-to-face or I'd spread the word that he was a pencil dick. He scratched his cheek and opened his door. He stepped outside. The screen door slammed.

I whirled and put my gun to his head. I spoke low with the intensity of a blade cutting through steel.

"Listen good, motherfucker. If you ever say another bad word about my father, I'll come back here and blow your fucking brains out. You got that, you piece of shit?"

Stanley began to shiver. I yanked the hammer back on the gun. "You got that, you fuck?"

He nodded.

"What? I didn't hear you."

"I got it."

"*What*? What do you *got*?"

Stanley whimpered and pressed his eyes shut. "I'll never bad-mouth your father again, I swear."

"Fucking right, you fuck. And tomorrow, your daughter better apologize to my sister in front of everyone, or I'll come back here again. And I'll kill you."

I lowered the gun and shoved him against his house. He tripped and landed on his ass. I stared at him for a good ten seconds before I turned around and left.

I was shaking so much that I went straight home.

A few hours later, half-drunk and very pissed, Stanley staggered into Harvey's Back Room, where my uncle Marty held court every night at his table in the corner. Stanley shoved past a waitress and stormed over to my uncle. The bar became silent.

"Marty," Stanley said.

Marty glanced up at him. He didn't say a word.

"You hear me, *Marty*? I'm talking to you. Your nephew came over to my *house* and threatened me with a *gun*—"

My uncle held up his hand. Stanley stopped speaking. After a count of five, Marty spoke in a whisper. "You're a lucky man, Stanley."

Stanley waited for Marty to continue. When he didn't, he said loudly, "*I'm* lucky? How so?"

"You're lucky my nephew got to you and I didn't." Uncle Marty's eyes bore into Stanley's eyes like two lasers. "Because I would've killed you. Anything further happens, I will."

Stanley turned as white as vanilla ice cream, then lurched out of the bar.

Meanwhile, I was going crazy at home. I needed to get out, needed to calm down, needed a drink. I drove over to Harvey's Back Room. As I headed in, Uncle Marty came out. He grabbed me by the sleeve and pulled me away from the door.

"What's the matter with you?"

"You heard, huh?"

"Everybody heard. What'd you do? You put a gun to that douche bag's head?"

"I know. It was stupid. I shouldn't have done it."

"Damn right. You should've killed him."

I blinked. "You wanted me to shoot him?"

"You put a gun to a guy's head and you let him go? *Kill* him."

I thrust my hands into my pants pockets. I swallowed. "Uncle Marty . . ."

That's all I needed to say. Uncle Marty shook his head. "Can't do it, can you?"

"No," I said. "I can't."

Uncle Marty swatted me lightly on the cheek. I couldn't tell if he was relieved or disappointed.

"It's okay, Mark, not everyone's a killer," he said. "Next time pistol-whip him. Beat the crap out of him. Use the gun butt. It's almost as good as a hit. Not quite. Almost. Got that?"

This was school. The course was Gangster Intimidation 101. I was the student, Uncle Marty was the teacher, and I had flunked the midterm. There was always the final.

"All right," Uncle Marty said. "I'm late for my date."

Seemed like Uncle Marty had a date with a different woman every night. Beautiful, exotic women, women who were out of my league. Uncle Marty knew them all and they all knew Uncle Marty. He was dapper and slick, a prince of the underworld. He wore designer suits that were freshly pressed and never seemed to wrinkle. I watched him slide behind the wheel of his new car, the latest model Cadillac. He waved at me with one finger and drove off.

Among rounders and hoods and hustlers, Uncle Marty was the Man. I longed to be like him, to be that cool, that slick.

And I knew in the deepest part of me that no matter how hard I tried, I never would be.

The next morning at school, a group of seventh-grade girls gathered around my sister. One girl stepped forward and apologized for what had happened the day before. She was very sorry about what she had said about my sister's father and hoped that they could still be friends.

My sister told her to go fuck herself.

In the early 1970s, my favorite bar was the Virginian on Van Eiken Road, across from the rapid transit tracks. I drank there nightly with a group of rounders. My typical evening consisted of heavy drinking and heavy flirting with a pretty barmaid named Coleen. We never got past that no matter how hard I tried or how much I tipped.

The owner of the Virginian was a feisty woman named Annie Quinn. Annie smoked a pipe and spoke in a raspy, longshoreman's voice. I usually ate dinner at the Virginian and every so often, on nights when I was too drunk to drive, I'd shack up on a cot Annie kept in the back room. I maintained a running tab at the Virginian, the amount of which nearly beat what I paid in rent.

At the time, I had a sweet scam going with a guy named Monty who had a car leasing business. I would lease cars from him, take out the insurance, then steal the cars, strip them—making sure they were just short of being totaled—collect the insurance money, then put the cars back together so Monty could lease them all over again. I'd pick up between five and ten grand a car, a good score in the 1970s.

True to my nature, I'd strut into the Virginian with a wad of cash on me as if I was some Vegas high roller. Of course, within days, I'd be dead broke. The money would flitter through my fingers like dust. Best thing to do was forget about it. The best way to forget? Drink. And drink I would. I'd drink until I was drunk as a cartoon.

Early one morning I started to stagger out of the bar toward my car. Annie intercepted me. She wanted me to sleep on the cot. I didn't feel like it. I wanted a shower, wanted to get home. I promised her I'd take it slow. I actually felt fine. I might've felt a tiny bit fuzzyheaded. No big deal. Par for the course.

I got into my car and started to drive. I only had to deal with one tricky part and it came up right away: the sharp left out of the parking lot. I had to concentrate. Focus. I slowed way down, gripped the steering wheel with both fists, peered straight ahead. I gave the wheel a tug, whipped it left, eased up, and . . .

Ka thunk.

What the . . .?

KAAA THUNNKKK.

A terrifying CRUNCH groaned beneath my wheels.

And then the car died.

I sat dazed in the driver's seat.

What just happened? I must have had a blowout. Or maybe the battery gave out. Or . . .

I opened the door and looked down at the road.

Only there wasn't any road. Just two metal rows. With wood slats in between.

Metal *rows*? And then I realized what I had done.

I had driven onto the rapid transit tracks.

The car was stuck. Impaled. Immobile as a planter.

And then reality hit me like a slap across the face.

"YOU JUST DROVE YOUR CAR ONTO THE RAPID TRANSIT TRACKS."

Instantly, I was sober. I grabbed the car telephone I'd installed, called the bar, and told Annie what I'd done. She paused and then her gravelly voice exploded into a howl. She shouted something to the room. The dial tone echoed in my ear.

Then everything happened at once. A tow truck appeared out of the fog, lights flashing. The driver, a headless figure in a hood, sprayed his high beams over my car resting on the tracks. I heard a cackle and a demand for cash.

My fingers fumbled for my flimsy wallet. Empty. I offered to write him a check. A hooded laugh blowing a breath cloud into my face. No cash, no tow, no check, no way.

I called the bar again and Annie picked up before the phone even rang and this time there were no words, just laughter, her hard-edged ha ha ha cranking into a hacking smoker's cough. And then, *whoosh*. Cops. Two of them. Burly white guys. Cleveland's finest, escorting me out of my car, onto the side of the road, making me walk a straight line and blow up some stupid fucking balloon and then I'm sitting in the backseat of the cop car, fumes from bad coffee circling my head.

Coleen pulled up in Annie's car. She was wearing a man's coat and trying to keep a straight face. She talked to the tow truck driver, handed him some money, then she peered into the back, casing my face.

A cop asked, "You taking him home?"

"You're not gonna arrest him?"

"You kidding?" the cop said. "This is the funniest thing we've seen on our beat in fifteen years."

They started laughing again, and Coleen cracked a smile. I couldn't help myself; I started to roar. We sat there, Coleen, the cops, and I laughing hysterically as the tow truck driver hooked a chain to my rear bumper, dragged my car off the tracks, and deposited it with a clatter into the middle of the road, which made us laugh even louder. Finally, the cops pulled away. I drove my car down a side street and climbed into Coleen's car with her. We headed back to the Virginian, where I took a whole lot of abuse from Annie and the rounders who were still there, and Annie made me buttermilk pancakes and some real coffee.

Then I went home with Coleen.

I drifted from job to job. I sold aluminum siding, cut and hung gutters, washed out empty metal drums that stored ice cream, worked in retail, sold cars. In general, I was an erratic employee. I was restless, unreliable, late. Often I was hungover or drunk. After a while, I could find only dead-end or dangerous jobs that nobody else wanted, like working in a junkyard disassembling discarded car engines in order to recycle the parts.

One day, I was pulling apart an engine and a warm liquid spilled on my left hand. My hand stung briefly. I wiped my fingers on my jeans and kept working. A few hours later, after work, my middle finger began to burn and swell and turn green. My mother made an appointment with a hand specialist she'd heard about through the temple. When I got to the doctor's office, the nurse said he wouldn't see me because I didn't have any insurance. I showed her my hand, which had turned a sickening shade of black. She told me to go immediately to the Mount Sinai Hospital emergency room in downtown Cleveland.

The emergency room was packed, mostly with gunshot victims. After a two-hour wait, a doctor examined my hand. He picked up a wall phone and barked into it. Within seconds, I was wheeled into an operating room.

The surgery took longer than anyone expected. My mother feared that I would lose my middle finger. When I woke up in recovery, my hand was wrapped in a bandage the size of a catcher's mitt. Lying next to me, a young black man howled and begged for drugs. Both of his hands were bandaged. He had been in a knife fight and had tried to fight off the other guy's knife with his bare hands. He had over a hundred stab wounds and he was crying and he was terrified.

My mother sat at the foot of his bed and wiped his forehead with a damp washcloth.

I didn't lose my finger. The acid from the car engine ate away the nail, leaving the middle finger of my left hand permanently disfigured.

In retrospect, I caught a break. At the time, I looked at the mangled tip of my middle finger and I saw what I believed was a symbol, a sign that the world was telling me, "Fuck you."

4

Checks, No Balances

I was a thief. Every thief uses a weapon, usually a gun or a knife. My weapon of choice was a checkbook.

Someone once told me that as long as you have a check, you'll never go broke. It's true. I discovered this early on when I first forged my mother's signature on a check and watched the bank teller count out five crisp ten-dollar bills right in front of me. I smiled, she smiled, and I walked away. Forging checks was a lot easier and more lucrative than stealing a wad of ones from my mother's purse.

I began to devise more elaborate scams. The simplest, of course, was writing a check from my account and bouncing it. Sometimes I'd make it good, sometimes I wouldn't. I *meant* to make it good. I just wouldn't get around to it or I'd forget about it or I'd be too drunk to move or too pissed off to bother.

Other times I'd open an account in a bank in another city or even another state, and a second account in a bank in Cleveland. I'd put a hundred dollars in each account. Then I'd write a check for a large amount, say $2,500, from the out of town account and deposit it in the city account. The next day I'd write a check for cash out of the city account for $2,000. Back then, it took two weeks for a check to clear from an out of city bank. I'd get to know the people at the banks in Cleveland, get them to recognize me. I'd bullshit with the guy tellers about sports and flirt with the female tellers. They never checked picture IDs, never wrote down license numbers, and they had no problem cashing my $2,000 check. This was called a float. Also known as check kiting or splitting. All fancy names for *stealing*.

I was living a dream. Nothing was real. I was a character in my own life, a gangster, a high roller with a bulging billfold. Nothing made sense so I'd drink to shut out the real world. I didn't want to have to deal with reality. Even when reality reared its ugly head at me time and time again. Like when I'd get fired from job after job because I was drinking, coming in late, fucking off. Or when I'd beat someone in my family. I didn't care. One time the mail came and there was a credit card addressed to my brother Neal, who was away at college. I took the credit card, activated it, and started banging out cash. I didn't care if I was running up a mountain of debt and that my mother was the one who would get stuck. Did, not, care.

I wasn't the good Jewish boy she thought I was. That was a myth. That was her dream, not mine. I couldn't stand the thought of winding up stuck in a Jewish suburb with a dead-end job, a nagging wife who belonged to the synagogue Sisterhood, and a house full of screaming little kids. That wasn't me. I wasn't going to end up being an ice cream maven like my cousin, even though he invited me to be his partner. Ben, Jerry, and Mark? Never.

My mother found out about my drinking the hard way. One New Year's Eve, when I was drunk out of my head, I borrowed my aunt Nettie's car and drove it into a tree. I walked away with a couple of bruises and scratches. The car was totaled, and my mother was beside herself.

She found out about my check writing a few weeks later when the bank called her and told her that her account was overdrawn by several hundred dollars. She didn't understand. My mother balanced her checkbook meticulously every month. She knew what she had to the penny. Her hands quivering on the steering wheel, she drove to the bank. A bank officer sat her down in his office and pulled out a stack of checks, all of them made out to cash, all bad, all forged by me. My mother recognized my handwriting. She lowered her head and in the bank officer's cubicle, she began to cry. He lowered the blinds.

Eventually, I paid her back. My mother didn't know how to react to me. When she saw me, she turned cold. She couldn't help herself. She felt pummeled with emotion. What I had done was beyond the scope of her imagination. It was as if I was a stranger living in her house. She did not recognize the man I had become. She did not know who I was.

I can understand that.

I didn't know who I was either.

My drinking made me reckless. I beat people I loved, destroyed relationships with people who cared about me. I loved my two uncles, Harry and Marty, and I beat them both. Can't tell you why. I just lashed out at everybody.

My uncle Harry's brother, Jack, owned a bar. It was a wild place. Drew a very tough crowd. My uncle Harry's friend Richie was the bartender. Richie was a rough customer himself. He carried a gun. The bar became a notorious bad guy hangout. Richie poured drinks, served food, booked bets, and for a small fee, he also cashed checks.

One night I gave Richie a check for five hundred dollars. He cashed it for me, no problem. The check, of course, was bad. I knew it was bad and I had every intention of making it good before it cleared.

Guess it slipped my mind. Or I had the money one day and didn't have it the next. Or . . .

I don't know. I just beat Richie.

He was not happy. He came after me when the check bounced. Uncle Harry stepped between us.

"He forgot to write it down, Richie," he said. "Ain't that right, Mark?"

I said nothing.

"Mother*fucker*," Richie said. "You beat me for five hundred in my own bar?"

"It was a mistake," Uncle Harry said. "You gotta write it down, Mark. You do so many things. He does a lot of things, Richie. It's hard to keep track. He forgets. He's gonna start writing everything down. Aren't you, Mark?"

I stared right at Richie.

"Yeah," I said. "Sure."

Richie couldn't hold my stare. He looked at my uncle Harry. "I don't give a shit if he writes it down or not. I want my money."

I paid Richie back the next day. Probably wrote somebody else a bad check to pay him off. I floated so many checks over Cleveland . . . it was like confetti.

I never cashed another check in that bar. From then on, whenever I looked at my uncle Harry, I could feel a small sadness coming from him. He was always there for me, always, even after I beat Richie. He knew I was fucking up, knew I was drinking, and he wanted to help me, he desperately wanted to help me. He just didn't know how, didn't know what to do. I hurt him, I know. Because whenever

I looked at him, I would see that ache, and I knew that I had broken his heart.

Late in 1974, my uncle Marty got nailed for stock fraud. I didn't know the details. Uncle Marty and I always kept our shit separate. This time he called me.

"I'm in a jam, Mark," he said. "I have to turn myself in. I don't want to spend one fucking minute in jail. I need a bond. Can you do it for me?"

"Sure, Uncle Marty."

I went to a guy I knew and got Uncle Marty a bond. He avoided jail and everything seemed fine.

Except I gave the bondsman a bad check.

It was as if I had sent out a boomerang and it had flown right back into my face. Uncle Marty had to talk to yet another guy to fix it up. He did. It all got straight.

For the time being.

The reason I left Cleveland can be summed up in two words.

Naugahyde tablecloths.

I had just turned twenty-five. I was dead broke and I couldn't find a job. I was combing the classifieds one day and came across an ad for a traveling salesman. I knew right away it was a hustle. Something about it smelled. That's what intrigued me. I called the number. They hired me over the phone.

My job was to convince restaurants to rent a month's supply of Naugahyde tablecloths. Naugahyde actually made sense because it was a dream to clean. All you had to do was wipe it off with a damp rag. That's it. Done. You saved a fortune in dry cleaning and freed up storage space, and Naugahyde came in several attractive designs and colors.

I answered to two bosses, posers who tried to appear tough and slick. One guy was tall and stoop-shouldered, sported an Elvis pompadour, and wore sunglasses, even inside. The other guy was shorter and thicker and liked to suck on toothpicks. I didn't see where the scam came in, which meant it came in everywhere. Which meant they'd try to scam me, too.

I hit the ground running. Lined up a dozen restaurants the first week. When I got my paycheck, I stared at it for thirty seconds before I flung it across the room. The two bastards had shorted me on both my draw and my expenses. I calmly brought the matter to their attention. They claimed that the restaurants hadn't all paid yet. They promised to make it up the following week. They deeply regretted the error in my expenses. They'd just hired a new bookkeeper and she was learning their system.

I decided to give them the benefit of the doubt. Allow them to get their bookkeeping in order. Straighten out the glitches. My second paycheck came. They shorted me again.

I expressed concern. They were *so* apologetic. They asked for my patience, especially since they'd fired the bookkeeper and were breaking in a new one. They promised to send me expense money while I was on the road and to pay my mother directly to help her cover the rent.

The third paycheck came. Same result.

Now I was pissed. I phoned my employers. I was cordial. I was understanding. I offered a solution: provide me with a company credit card to use for expenses. It would be easier and more efficient.

The two morons bought it.

They gave me a Visa card.

My first move was to ditch the job and take off for New York. I checked into a suite at the Plaza, charged three hundred bucks' worth of room service and found a high-class hooker who took plastic. The next night I went barhopping and met up with a maniac gangster from Florida who got me into what seemed like a foolproof get-rich-quick scam. After I banged out a couple more New York nights on the company credit card, we flew down to Florida to work his con. I checked into the Fountainbleau, gorged myself on expensive food and women, and finished off my business with the maniac, who, it turned out, was on the lam from the law. He made himself scarce, I pumped one more night out of my charge card, then headed back to work hawking Naugahyde tablecloths.

By the time I got back to Cleveland, the credit card statement had come in and Elvis and Toothpick were beyond pissed. I had slammed out about five grand's worth of fun and games for myself. They wanted their money back. Said they were withholding my paycheck until I paid them. We hit an impasse. I attempted to clarify how I stood on the matter.

"I quit," I said.

"You beat us for five grand," Elvis said.

"We want our money," Toothpick said.

"Go fuck yourselves," I said.

"Hey," Toothpick said. A threat.

"By the way," I said. "Those Naugahyde tablecloths? They're sticky, they're ugly, and they smell like shit."

"Yeah?" Elvis said. Another threat.

"Yeah," I said. "Hey, I have an idea. Why don't you fold one up and shove it up your ass?"

I probably shouldn't have said that. Because the two dickheads started calling my house and threatening my mother and my sister.

They called early in the morning, they called late at night. They threatened to hurt them if I didn't pay them back.

I called a cousin of mine and told him what was going down. He offered to go through the credit card statement and settle the charges that were obviously personal.

"I can't let you do that," I said.

"Mark, it's the only way to keep those guys from calling your house."

"I don't have the money to pay you back."

"We're family," he said.

He sent them a check for a third of the expenses.

It wasn't enough. They wanted all of it. They kept calling my house. The threats got worse. Sicker. More violent. They'd call all through the night. My mother was a wreck. My sister was freaking out.

I wanted to hunt them down, wanted to blow their fucking brains out. I knew I couldn't. I felt helpless. I didn't know what to do, whom to turn to. I couldn't talk to Uncle Harry. He would just get upset. Uncle Marty was gone, behind bars or on the run. I felt that everyone else had turned his back on me.

One day I got a message to go to a place called the Bluegrass, a well-known mob hangout. The message was from Tony Damiano, Cleveland underboss and my adopted godfather. The message said it was urgent.

The Bluegrass was a dark bar. A row of ceiling fans hung low, whirring in slow, smoky circles. I walked in and tried to adjust my eyes to the dim light. I finally identified Tony. He was sitting by himself in a booth in the back. Tony was never alone. I knew that three or four of his crew were sitting nearby in the dark. As I walked toward him, I could hear invisible throats clearing. It had been a year or so since I'd seen Tony. He was as dapper as always. He wore a monstrous pinkie ring that flashed like a beacon.

He gestured for me to sit. I lowered myself into the booth

and sat across from him. Tony smelled of strong cologne. His white hair was sculpted back into a hard sheen.

"You really pissed off a couple of guys," he said. Tony offered me a cigarette from a gold case. I took one. A hand reached out of the darkness and flicked open a lighter. A flame shot up. I bent over and lit my cigarette. I blew the smoke up and watched it snake up into a ceiling fan.

"They are not pleased," Tony said.

"They're assholes, Tony. They're calling my house, threatening my mother, my sister."

Tony winced as if he had swallowed something sour.

"I wanted to take care of it myself," I said. "I didn't want to bother you with this—"

Tony sliced his hand across the table. He looked like an umpire giving the safe sign. I stopped talking. Tony leaned onto his elbows.

"These guys want to kill you," he said. "They want me to authorize a hit. They're meeting me here in a half hour. They're bringing ten grand."

"Ten grand to have me hit?"

Tony squeezed out a laugh. "Too much or too little?"

I sucked another drag off my cigarette, then looked around for someplace to punch it out. The same hand appeared and plopped an ashtray down on the table.

"Tell me what happened," Tony said.

I told him everything. Told him about the stupid, ugly Naugahyde tablecloths, told him about getting stiffed on my paycheck and expenses, about running up the company credit card, and about how my cousin had tried to settle. When I finished, Tony opened his mouth slightly and let out a small click. Then he smoothed his palms along the sides of his hair, as though he were applying hair tonic.

"These two guys have done some work for me. Strictly small-time. Still, they bring me a beef, I gotta listen."

I shrugged.

"They threatened your mother?"

"And my sister. They call the house all night long. My mother's a fucking wreck."

"Awright." Tony made the clicking sound again. "I want you to sit over there."

Tony tilted his head toward the far corner of the room. I squinted in that direction. In the blackness, I could barely see the outline of a table.

"When I flash my ring, come back over here and sit down next to me."

"Okay," I said.

Tony pressed his hands together in front of his mouth, forming a miniature steeple. It looked as if he might say a prayer. This was my signal. I stood up and walked off into the darkness.

Twenty minutes later Elvis and Toothpick walked in, escorted by two guys I recognized from Mario's. Elvis had abandoned his sunglasses for the occasion and Toothpick's bottom lip was bare. They looked naked. Tony took a sip from his water glass and motioned for them to sit down. They scrambled into the booth.

"We brought the money," Elvis said.

"Ten grand," Toothpick said.

Elvis nodded and Toothpick produced a bulging mailing envelope. He held it in the air for a split second. The disconnected hand materialized and snatched the envelope out of the air. Nobody spoke. In the darkness, I heard the rustling of crisp new bills being counted.

"It's all here," a voice said.

And then Tony flashed his pinkie ring.

I stepped out of the shadows and slid into the booth next to Tony Damiano.

"I believe you've met," Tony said. Again, the *click*.

Elvis and Toothpick simultaneously sank back in the booth, causing the red vinyl seat to squish. Elvis's eyes darted around the room. Toothpick craned his neck to the right, casing the place, searching for an escape route.

"Surprise," I said.

Tony raised an eyebrow at me, a warning to shut my mouth.

"He fucked us," Elvis mumbled.

"Let me correct you," Tony said. "You got *beat*. By a twenty-five-year-old kid. And you're pissed off."

Toothpick cupped his palm and moved it back and forth from his chest toward Tony.

"We thought," he said. He swallowed and tried again. "Tony, you know, we *thought*."

"Tony," said Elvis. A plea.

Tony put an arm around my shoulder. "Did you know that Mark is my adopted godson?"

Then, to make that point, Tony Damiano, Cleveland mob underboss, kissed me on the cheek. He turned back to Elvis and Toothpick. "I love him like a son. Anything happens to him, he gets a cut, a scratch, he catches a *cold* . . . I'm holding you two responsible."

Elvis's lower lip dropped. "Tony, we didn't know."

"We really didn't," Toothpick said.

"How could you?" Tony said.

"It was an honest mistake," Elvis said.

Tony nodded, removed his arm from my shoulder, and

leaned into the two morons across from him. "This ends here and now. No more threatening phone calls. Nothing. Is that understood?"

"Absolutely," Elvis said.

"Definitely," Toothpick said.

"This meeting is over," Tony said.

Elvis and Toothpick shot up as if they'd been catapulted from an ejector seat. They pushed their way out of the booth. Elvis suddenly whirled around. He bent over toward Tony as though he were taking a bow.

"Tony, the ten grand . . . since it's a no-go, I was wondering, you know, if we could, um, have it, back—"

"What ten grand?" Tony said.

Elvis and Toothpick froze. A veil of *ill* slid down each of their faces like a window shade. A flurry of heavily muscled arms appeared out of the shadows, and my former employers were guided out of the bar like two blind men.

I turned to Tony to thank him. He ducked away from my eyes, then abruptly looked back at me. I could feel a black breeze in the room. Tony fumbled in his back pocket and yanked out a monogrammed handkerchief. He dabbed his eyes, then blew his nose. He sniffed. He paused, then looked me over. His eyes were watery.

"You're getting sloppy," he said. His voice was hoarse.

I spread out my hands and pressed my palms into the table. Then Tony said in a flat whisper, "Maybe you should consider relocating."

Neither of us spoke for a long time. Finally I said, "My brother's in California."

"Nice out there," Tony said. "Warm."

Tony stood up and awkwardly sidestepped out of the

booth. I met him at the edge of the table. We hugged and kissed each other on both cheeks and then I walked out of the bar. Three days later, I left for Los Angeles.

I spent the next two days packing my things and saying my good-byes. I hit all the bars and said good-bye to Annie and John and all the other bartenders who'd taken my phone messages, cooked me food when I was broke, and in Annie's case, given me a cot to sleep off more than one bender. I said good-bye to my cousins, aunts, and uncles, ate dinner with them, and played gin rummy into the night.

I spent a couple of hours at the barbershop with Mario. We talked about guys we knew who were either big shots in the mob because they were quick and cool or in the joint or dead because they were stupid or unlucky. We talked about Mario's career in radio. He lamented that he could've been another Jack Benny. He just never got a break. We listened to a couple of tapes from the old shows. He gave me a bottle of good vodka as a going-away present. We hugged, a solemn, lingering embrace.

After Mario's, I drove to the Heights Temple. I didn't go in. I parked outside and sat in my car, remembering the time I was turned away because I didn't have a High Holiday ticket. I remembered, too, how I prayed with the old men and how I fit in with them, even though I was young enough to be one of their grandchildren.

The morning of the third day I said good-bye to my mother.

"Maybe a change of scenery will do you good," she said.

"I think so," I said. "And I'll be able to look after Stuart."

Life had recently taken a toll on my brother. His wife had

left him and he'd been diagnosed with MS. And from what I could determine by talking to him on the phone, he'd gone into the jewelry business with a pretty unsavory character. Poor Stuart. He was a good guy who never could catch a break.

"You'll live with Stuart?" my mother asked.

"Yes. For a while anyway," I said.

My mother nodded. We didn't say much more.

"You'll come back once in a while," she said after a while. It was more of a wish than a question.

"Definitely," I said.

We hugged. Neither of us tried to pull away.

"Don't worry, Ma," I said as I held her. My words brushed her hair. "Everything's gonna be different in California. You'll see. Everything's gonna be different."

She held me tighter, and I could feel her tears streaming down her cheeks, dripping into mine.

Finally, on my way out of town, I drove to the cemetery and said good-bye to my father.

It was mid-February 1977, bitterly cold, as frigid a morning as I'd ever felt in Cleveland. The sky was gray and filthy. The air stung. It had snowed the night before and the ground was a treacherous sheet of ice. I took small, tentative steps as I slid toward my father's grave. I reached his headstone and I planted myself in front. I folded my gloved hands.

"Oh, Dad," I said. I lowered my head. "Why did you have to die? Tell me. Why did you have to *die*?"

I shoved my hands into my jacket pocket. My nose started to run.

"My life . . . my fucking *life*."

Suddenly, I was gasping for air. I felt as if I was trapped underwater. I steadied myself, took a deep breath, and then

I started to cry. With tears flowing down my face, I bent over and I found a pebble. I laid the pebble on my father's head-stone and I stood at the foot of his grave and I just lost it.

"Why? Tell me *why*? I don't understand. I don't *under-stand*. I don't know what to do, please tell me what to do. I don't know who I am. *Oh God, I don't know who I am.*"

I turned and ran out of the cemetery. I stumbled and I tripped. I picked myself up and I crashed over the slick frozen ground and I got into my car and, with tears burning my eyes and half-blinding me, I left for California.

5

Hollywood Hustle

I pulled up in front of my brother's apartment complex on February 22, 1977. It was seventy degrees and sunny and there were palm trees swaying in a cool, lazy breeze. Three days before, I was living in Ice Station Zebra. Here I was, in Paradise.

Stuart lived in a two-bedroom apartment a half block from the center of Alhambra, a mostly Latino suburb of L.A. at the eastern edge of the San Fernando Valley. Alhambra's main street was as wide as the Ohio Turnpike and lined with car dealerships, cheap Mexican restaurants, dark bars, seedy strip clubs, and liquor stores that sold the *Racing Form*. My kind of town.

The apartment was clean and furnished with the kind of drab furniture you'd find in a Motel 6. The complex had everything I needed: a laundry room, Ping-Pong table, soda machine, and swimming pool. Alhambra got hot, desert hot, and there was nothing more refreshing than a dip before dinner or, in my case, a cannonball before a con. I'd shower after my evening plunge and head out to my favorite bar, slapping my cheeks with English Leather to cut the smell of the chlorine.

To get on my feet, I worked for my brother and his partner, a pseudo tough guy from Detroit. Me and this guy? Dislike at first sight. He was pompous and loud and had a way of talking out of the corner of his mouth like he knew every angle. He didn't know shit. My brother, though, revered him. I had the sense that Nathan Detroit was stealing my brother blind. I couldn't prove it and I didn't want to bad-mouth him to Stuart. I was here five minutes and wasn't about to rock the boat.

My brother and Nathan worked as manufacturer's reps for a couple of different jewelry lines, and they hired me to write and refill orders around L.A. and the San Fernando Valley. I didn't know much about jewelry and even less about L.A. I used this as an opportunity to learn the landscape, both geographical and criminal. It didn't take me long. After a few months, I worked for them and hustled on the side. I'd buy my own jewelry, using bad checks of course, and sell gold and bronze in bars.

By this time, living with my brother had pretty much turned to shit. We were arguing constantly, mostly over money and his dumb fuck of a partner, and we were not getting along. For his health and my sanity, I decided to look for my own place.

I found a furnished two-bedroom in Tarzana on Reseda Boulevard, a shot glass toss from the best bars and restaurants in the West Valley. To make a totally clean break, I quit working for my brother and his crazy partner and took a job selling and leasing used BMWs.

I found a perfect partner, a bank that would take any kind of paper I'd give them. If a customer was interested in a lease, I'd make it work. Got bad credit, no credit, no job, no money? No problem. I'd make it stick. For some reason, people wanted those used Beemers more than anything in the world. They'd put up their house, mortgage their firstborn. They *had* to have those cars. Well, I was creative, and the bank didn't care. They wanted to move money as much as I did.

And I'd do any size deal. I didn't have to hit a home run every time. You can score a lot of runs by hitting singles. I'd go for the deals that other guys would turn down because they seemed too small or too risky. I'd close any deal, any time, big, small, shaky or sure. A deal was a deal. Period.

The money started rolling in. Two, three, four thousand a month. And I spent it as fast as I earned it. The concept of *saving* eluded me. Never entered my brain. Or if it did, I just laughed it off. Savings accounts were for those Ozzie and Harriet types, boring dudes you'd see on TV. That was an America I never knew. A happy, wholesome America bathed in Technicolor, safe and secure behind a white picket fence. My America was a nation of shadows, of dark, desperate characters living on the run. Ozzie was a drunk, Ricky was a hustler, David was a con man, Harriet was a hooker.

I owned the night. I'd hole up at a bar called Heckles, blow my wad on steak dinners for the house, and try to hustle hot merchandise I'd bought with hot checks. I'd drink deep into the next morning, sleep and shower off my hangover, and stagger over to the car dealership for my afternoon shift. I had one goal in life: to get rich. I was so twisted. I worshipped money and I shit all over it.

I switched jobs. I wanted something closer to my apartment. I heard about an opening at a Datsun dealership five minutes away. I interviewed with the sales manager and got hired on the spot.

The used car manager there was a guy named Charlie Stein. Charlie was about ten years older than I was and a real character. He was tall and built like a bear. Charlie had a past. Back in the day, he'd done a stint in the federal pen. I think he did some state time, too, though he was pretty vague about that. Charlie's crime was dealing drugs. Cocaine. He was a New York guy who hung out with Italian gangsters. He was the real deal, a hard case if I ever saw one.

Charlie and I hit it off. We'd take our breaks together. We'd sit and smoke and drink coffee and swap mob stories. Charlie was a storyteller and a comedian and he loved to laugh. His laugh was like a thunderclap. He'd roar and shake all over as if he were having some sort of fit.

Charlie played every angle. He'd package a solid deal with a shaky deal, which would force the lot manager to go for both. At the same time, he was being paid off by the used car wholesalers, which meant he was getting a piece of the action on both ends. He blatantly tried to steal trades from all the salesmen he worked with, including me. He was shameless.

One time, he gave me an outrageously low bid on a car. I decided to call him on it. I phoned my cousin who was also a car wholesaler and told him to meet me at the lot. I wanted to show him a car. My cousin drove over, checked out the car, and offered me five hundred dollars more than Charlie had. I bypassed Charlie, went directly to my sales manager, and made the deal with my cousin. Charlie was pissed. He confronted me in the break room.

"Why the fuck did you do that?" Charlie stood over me. His face turned a freaky shade of purple.

I walked up to him and stuck my nose an inch away from him. "Listen, asshole. I don't care what you do with all those other guys. That's their business. However, you are not going to fuck with me on these trades. I'm done with that shit."

I was ready to go at it then and there.

Charlie stared at me for a few seconds, then he started to

laugh, the full body rumble, and he said in a soft whisper, "Okay, so on yours I'll give you the right number."

From then on, Charlie and I were fast friends. He never screwed me again, and I got him to start doing business with my cousin. Charlie and I became partners. I always had some scheme. I wanted to get into used car leasing again. At first, Charlie was against it.

"Nobody wants to lease a used car. You're wasting your time."

"Let me run an ad," I told him. "I can get people into used Nissans, believe me."

"It'll never work."

"Give me one good reason."

"Okay. You're an ignorant motherfucker. Want another reason?"

"Listen, dickhead, let me worry about getting the paper down. You just get the cars. If it works, we both win."

"It'll never work," he said.

It worked. We began blowing out used cars. At one point, the two of us were leasing more cars than the entire in-house leasing department. Charlie never second-guessed me again.

In December 1978, I started drinking at a joint called the Sugar Mill. I met a guy there named Ron. We called him the Cowboy because he always wore a cowboy hat and cowboy clothes, and he drove a Ranchero. The Cowboy introduced me to one of the all-time best scams.

The idea was to call up veterinarians and chiropractors and arrange to buy their old X-ray film. Every year or so they'd dump their old film and buy a new supply. The Cowboy told me that from X-rays, you could get silver. I'd buy up all this old X-ray film, bundle it together, and take it to a processing plant. The plant would pay me according to the going rate for silver. This scam made me a small fortune. And it didn't cost me a penny because I bought the old X-ray film with bad checks.

Sometimes I'd do a float, one account to another. Most of the time I'd give the vets and chiropractors a bad check from a fake company. I'd either get company checkbooks from companies that were out of business or I'd make up my own phony company, print a few checks, and open a business account with a hundred bucks.

It was beautiful. I'd show up at some vet, say I was Mark from Unique Enterprises, write a bad check for two hundred pounds of X-ray film, head over to the silver processing plant, sell the film to them, and walk out with a lump of cash. After they realized I'd beat them, I'm sure the banks and vets tried to find me by calling the phony phone number on the phony check I'd given them or locating the address of Unique Enterprises, which, of course, didn't exist. I was tempted to name one of my companies URFKD Inc. The Cowboy talked me out of it.

One night I got a call from one of my cousins from Cleveland. He told me my uncle Marty had suffered a heart attack in Chicago. Uncle Marty was always on the road, playing it fast and loose with hustles and women. He didn't know where to turn. I called him and invited him to move in with me. He didn't think twice about it. Within the week, he'd moved into my second bedroom.

I almost didn't recognize him. He was a shell of himself.

He had gotten old. He seemed used up. The hustler's life can take its toll. You're constantly on the short end of cash flow and always looking over your shoulder, making sure you're one step ahead of your marks and the law. Eventually, the life catches up to you. It didn't occur to me, of course, that when I looked at Uncle Marty I could be looking into an older, mirror image of myself.

Marty hid out in my apartment. His hustling days were coming to an end. He wasn't bringing in any cash, and I didn't ask him to contribute to the rent, which I forgot to pay half the time anyway. Marty was family. He was my father's brother. I loved him and I owed him and I tried my best to take care of him, even though I had a hard enough time taking care of myself.

When management at the Datsun dealership found out how much Charlie Stein was taking them for, they canned him. Charlie didn't care; he was bored there anyway. He wanted to branch out. He was itching to get into bigger plays, shit that was way too heavy-duty for me. He made me offers. I passed. He hit the road, vanished from sight. I knew we'd hook up eventually. We had one of those relationships. We were destined to cross paths again.

After Charlie left, I moved over to Victory Ford, a place we called Felony Ford because everyone who worked there seemed to have been convicted of a felony. The owners, Jimbo Hammer and Wally Dunlop, were as dirty as you could be. To this day, I believe they were mobbed up and the dealership was a front. They were into so much *shit*. I didn't know half of it. I know they were into the boxing scene. They owned fighters. Years later, something went bad with one of their boxers. I never knew the details. My guess is a fix was in and the message didn't get communicated properly. One night Wally drove off the lot to go home and he never showed up. He was found the next morning in the trunk of his car. His face had been beaten to a bloody pulp. The cops never found his killer.

I began my stint at Felony Ford and settled in to a routine. I had my favorite bars and I'd do the circuit—Tracton's, Chevy's, the Ram's Horn. I'd hit one joint and drink with the Cowboy, buy him a round, head over to another place, hang out with a couple of football players (L.A. had the Rams then), buy them a round, move to Tracton's, buy myself a steak dinner, and maybe bring home a barmaid. Weekends I'd fly to Vegas, blow a load on football and craps, come home broke, get a loan from Wally or Jimbo, sell a couple of cars, float a few checks, get the cash, drink, go back to Vegas, blow the cash, and begin my week all over again. If I'd had any vision, I'd have seen I was living in a circle, and the beginning and the end were exactly the same place.

I tried to look after Uncle Marty. He needed more than I could give him, needed more than a binged-out, busted nephew, and one night he was gone. He landed in an apartment in the company of a woman he'd met somewhere. She helped nurse him back to health, enabling him to resume the hustling life, a life he continued to live for the rest of his days, of which there were few.

In the meantime, I moved or got evicted, I don't remember which, and I was living here and there, back at my brother's place, on my cousin's couch, in some barmaid's bed, in the spare room of a friend, in the Cowboy's camper. My home phone was the number of a bar, my mail was sent to Mail Boxes Etc.

One afternoon, after a light lunch of a steak sandwich, fries, and two double manhattans, I headed over to Felony Ford for my three o'clock shift. As I approached an intersection two blocks away, I saw Jimbo standing on the street corner. He caught my eye and started waving at me like a third-base coach sending the runner. I couldn't figure out what the hell he was doing. It didn't dawn on me that he wanted me to turn around until I got to the next intersection and saw Mike, the used car sales manager, standing on that corner. He began frantically rotating his arms in a circle like a windmill gone wild.

I drove past Felony and pulled into a gas station. I got out and called the dealership from a pay phone. Wally answered.

"Mark, where are you?"

"Around the corner, Wally. What's going on?"

"The heat's here. They're looking for you."

I was stunned. I stumbled over my next sentence. "Why . . . what are you talking about?"

"The cops, man. Two of 'em are sitting in your office. They said they've been looking for you for weeks. You're slippery, Mark. They have no clue where you live. They got a list of the bars you hang out at. They kept missing you so they came here."

"Shit. What's their beef?"

"They want to talk to you about some checks."

I was busted. And I was pissed off. Getting arrested was an annoyance. It was in my way.

And it made me feel legitimate.

As twisted as that sounds, getting busted validated me. I was a bad guy after all. I always talked the talk. Now I could walk the walk. I had a bust next to my name. It made me feel big.

I had to post a bond. I wasn't sure how to do it. I called the one person I knew who could help me. The phone rang four times before he picked up.

"Hello?" His radio voice was only a slight bit thinner.

"Hey, Mario."

"Mark? I don't believe it! Where are you?"

Someone laughed in the background, and the bell tinkled over the door as someone else came in. I squeezed my eyes shut. I could almost smell the hair tonic in the barbershop.

"I'm in L.A."

"What's the weather like, Mark?"

"Seventy degrees and sunny."

"Here it's dark and cold. Expecting snow."

I smiled. I always told people it was seventy degrees and sunny. Today it was a hundred degrees and the smog was making my eyes tear.

"Mario, I'm in a jam." He waited. "I need a bond."

Mario cleared his throat. "You have to call a woman named Rhonda Coben. You know her?"

"No."

"Her husband is Paulie Morelli."

That name I knew. Paulie Morelli was a higher-up in the L.A. Mafia. He was originally from Cleveland. Mario used to cut his hair. I used to shine his shoes.

"Paulie will remember you," Mario said.

"I was a kid," I said.

"Paulie will remember you," Mario said again.

"Thanks, Mario." I was impatient to get the bond and get on with my life. I had business to do. Shit to sell, bad checks to write, people to beat.

"You in a hurry, Mark?"

"Well, yeah, Mario, you know—"

"*Mark.*" Mario spit my name back at me. "You get the bond, you can stop. You can stop it all now. Pick up the pieces and start over. You hear what I'm saying?"

"I hear you. Believe me I hear you. That's why I'm calling. I want to put an end to this—"

"The fuck you do." Mario let the words hang. I switched hands on the phone, then pressed the cool face of the receiver against my other ear. I did not want to have this conversation.

"No, I do," I said.

"Listen to me," Mario said. "You're a smart kid. This road you're on? It's the road to hell. You hear me? You do not want to go down this road. Because once you do, you can't turn around. Understand me? You gotta turn around now. You gotta stop *now.*"

"I hear you," I said. "Thanks, Mario."

I didn't hear him. And I didn't stop.

Hell had just begun.

My brother and I entered Rhonda Coben's Bail Bonds, a storefront in Van Nuys, tucked into a block of pawnshops, massage parlors, liquor stores, and five-dollar psychics. Rhonda met us at the counter. She was a formerly good-looking woman who had put on weight and dyed her big hair the color of a canary. She eyed my brother and me as if she were a casting a porno movie. My brother was there to sign the $15,000 bond, which was the biggest joke of all since he didn't have fifteen cents.

"I need a bond," I told her. "I don't have any collateral. I can give you ten percent now."

She snickered and stuffed a pencil into her hair.

"Who do you think you are?"

"I'm Mark Borovitz from Cleveland. Call Paulie. He knows what's going on."

She studied me, then tugged an old rotary phone over to her by the cord. She plucked the pencil out of her hair and used it to dial a number.

"Hey, Paulie," she said into the phone. "Guy here named Mark Borovitz. Says he's from Cleveland . . ."

That's all I heard from her end. She nodded a few times, tapped the counter with her pencil, smiled at my brother and winked at me. She hung up the phone, tilted her head, and patted the back of her hairdo as if it were a helmet.

"They sure love you in Cleveland," she said.

She wrote the bond.

The next morning, I surrendered myself to the police. As arranged by my attorney, I arrived at the Van Nuys police station at ten o'clock. A plainclothes cop, Officer Schell, waited outside the front door. She was a grim-faced woman with dark wavy hair and leathery skin. She reached into her pocket and pulled out a wad of checks as thick as a deck of cards. "These look familiar?"

I laughed in her face.

"You wrote all these, too, didn't you?"

Of course I had. I shook my head and gave her a wide-eyed, goofy grin.

"I have no idea what you're talking about," I said. "I'm a legitimate businessman."

Then, as if she were doing a magic trick, she whipped out a pair of handcuffs and slapped them over my wrists.

"What are you doing?" I said. "I'm surrendering myself."

"I consider you a flight risk," Schell said.

"Are you kidding me? I want to talk to my attorney."

Officer Schell shrugged. "He's not here. Let's go wait for him. Meantime I'd like to see how you write. You know how to write, don't you?"

She led me into a back office and asked me to copy a paragraph out of a book. The book was a dog-eared paperback copy of *In Cold Blood* by Truman Capote. Nice touch.

"This is bullshit," I said. "I don't know anything about those checks."

"Then what are you worried about?"

She looked at me. She had yellow eyes. Snake eyes the size of pinpricks. I grabbed a pen on the table in front of me and started copying a paragraph out of the book. She folded her arms and left the room.

I fucked around like mad. I printed some lines. Wrote backward on others. Wrote tiny cursive letters and scribbled large heavy letters. On one line, I used my left hand. Five minutes later, Officer Schell came back with my attorney. His name was Paul. He was a short fleshy guy with thick horn-rimmed glasses. He looked like an owl.

"You okay, Mark?"

"Oh yeah. I'm having *fun*. Officer Schell and I are really hitting it off." I leaned over to my lawyer and said in a stage whisper, "I think she kinda likes me."

He turned to her. "What are you holding my client in here for?"

"Let me answer that," I said. "Checks. A whole stack of checks that she shoved in my face. Checks that I have never seen before. I don't know what the hell she's talking about. Have no idea. She forced me to give a handwriting sample, too. Paul, I'm a businessman. I have clients waiting. If I weren't such a nice guy, I'd charge Officer Schell for my time. Take *her* to court."

I grinned at Officer Schell. She narrowed her yellow snake eyes and she sniffed. I expected her to flick out an alien tongue.

"Let's go, Mark," Paul said. "You're posting bond."

I got to my feet. "Very nice meeting you, Officer Schell," and just to be obnoxious, I bowed.

That really pissed her off. "He can't walk away. I want him locked up. He can't just bond right out!"

"Watch me, honey," I said.

I thought she would go for me then. Paul quickly steered me past her toward a desk where Rhonda Coben waited. As I signed a stack of smudged papers at warp speed, Officer Schell materialized by my elbow. She said, low, "I will see you again . . . *honey*."

She stormed off.

"Friend of yours?" Rhonda asked.

"Yeah. My girlfriend."

"I can tell." Rhonda stuffed the pen I was using into her big hair. "So Mark, we're at the Fireside most nights. Paulie would love to see you. I don't know if you're a drinking man . . ."

I shrugged. "On occasion."

"You posted bond," she said. "That's an occasion."

"Definitely," I said.

A Donna Summer song thrummed through a tinny overhead speaker as I sat in the Fireside's horseshoe-shaped corner booth with Rhonda and her husband, Paulie Morelli, a former fixture at Mario's. Paulie had a nervous, rodent face, which featured a jagged scar running the length of his left cheek. I'd seen him come through Mario's barbershop with a dozen women, none of them his wife. We were catching up.

"Ever hear from Benny Stefano?" I asked.

Paulie shrugged. "Lost track of him."

That meant he was dead.

"He ran with a guy," I said. "Big guy. Always wore an Indians' cap."

"Vinnie Bracco," Paulie said.

I snapped my fingers. "Yeah. Vinnie Bracco. He had good hair."

"Like a fucking golf course." Paulie drained his beer. "Lost track of him, too."

"Paulie lost touch with the old crew when we moved out here, know what I'm saying?" Rhonda said.

"Sure," I said.

"You make new associates," Paulie said.

"All the time," I said.

The front door opened and someone walked in. Paulie jerked his head toward the door and signaled with a raised pinkie.

"Business associate," he said. "Funny guy. You'll like him."

I stood up to make room in the booth for the newcomer. I turned and faced Charlie Stein.

"Shit," Charlie said, "they'll let anyone in here."

We pumped hands, and Charlie massaged my rapidly thinning patch of hair with his palm. He roared his rumble of a laugh, his whole body shaking.

"Guess you guys know each other," Paulie said.

"You kidding? It's Markie the Kid," Charlie said. "Keep one hand on your wallet, Paulie."

"What's it been, Charlie?" I asked.

"Coupla years. Been that long since I left Felony."

"How do you two know each other?" I asked Paulie.

"Charlie works for me in film distribution."

"Film distribution?"

"Yeah," said Charlie. "I sell pornos."

"The San Fernando Valley is the center of the whole industry," Rhonda said.

"Quite a distinction," I said.

"Well, New York's the Big Apple," Charlie said.

I said, "What's L.A., the Big Banana?"

Charlie roared again, his body convulsing until he finally got control of himself.

"Oh man," he said. "Hey, Paulie, some reason this month we got a lot of pirate pictures."

"Love those," Rhonda said.

"We got one . . . *Long Shlong Silver.* Excellent. Has a plot."

"Maybe you two should team up," Paulie said. "It's easy money, Mark."

"I don't know," I said. "Pornos."

"What, are you getting all moral on me? You work at *Felony* Ford," Charlie said.

I shrugged. "What the fuck."

I had a court case pending and the heat on my ass. Why not add selling illegal porno films to the list?

Sure. What the fuck.

By the end of the night, Charlie and I were once again partners in crime. We began by hustling pornos for Paulie Morelli, then we bought and sold truckloads of other stuff—microwaves, car telephones, TVs, VCRs—as well as dabbled in bank splitting schemes that we cooked up together. We were a constant, twenty-four/seven crime spree.

Charlie would do anything. Not me. There were certain crimes I wouldn't commit. Charlie made his biggest scores dealing drugs. I didn't want to go there. Oh, I dabbled. Didn't really dig it. There was no con, no sting, no sizzle, and to me, the rush was in the sizzle. I got my kicks conning people into buying stuff they didn't want.

Charlie also didn't mind violence. I drew the line there. I couldn't stand hurting people physically. No matter how hard Charlie sold me on some creepy nighttime ride involving a mobbed-up crew getting heavy, I'd back off. Not my style. Not my scene. And, frankly, those times soured me on Charlie. I wished he didn't have to go that far. I'd argue with him, try to convince him to hang out with me, hit the bars, have a few laughs. Usually he was too coked-out to listen. I guess running with a violent crew made Charlie feel tough or like one of the Boys. I just didn't need it as bad.

Soon after I got my legal affairs in order, I returned to Felony Ford. The moment I stepped onto the lot, Wally and Jimbo called me into their office.

"There's too much heat on you to stay here," Jimbo said. "The law starts getting their nose in too deep here, no telling what they'll find."

"Nothing personal," Wally said. "Sorry."

"You're letting me go? I'm getting fired from Felony Ford? That's gotta be a first."

"We're not firing you," Wally said. "You're relocating."

"We found a position for you up north," Jimbo said.

"We take care of our own. Hooked you up in 'Frisco," Wally said.

Jimbo thumbed a business card at me. "They're expecting you."

I took the card, flipped it through my fingers, and read the face. "Bay Mazda, huh? What do they call this, Misdemeanor Mazda?"

Wally and Jimbo laughed.

I left my head in San Francisco.

To me, the city felt like a Grateful Dead song—endless, formless, trippy, and mind-numbing. Everywhere I turned, people were doing drugs. I tried my share. They seemed to work in reverse. Pot hopped me up and killed my appetite. Downers made me fly, uppers made me crash. I gave up. My body was wired for booze. At parties in the Haight, I passed up the bong and wandered the district in search of a bar or liquor store, the lone leather jacket in a sea of-tie-dye.

I flew down to L.A. often. I had a court case pending, meetings with my lawyer, deals to make. I never stopped the hustle. Back in 'Frisco, I hooked up with Amy, a girl I knew from high school. She was dating a loser she'd met in the Bay Area, a flaked-out dope fiend with wild hair. Loser was into a series of scams, each one more lamebrained than the next. I decided to jump in and show them how a real gangster worked.

Amy and Loser knew a group of Asians who sold shit on the black market—cigarettes, drugs, appliances, anything they could get their hands on. I told Amy and Loser to make a deal with them. I knew two Italian brothers in L.A. who had access to the merchandise they wanted. I decided to play matchmaker. Why not? The Asians, Amy, and Loser got to play with the Big Boys while I got a nice cut for brokering the deal. Easy money and everybody wins.

Amy, Loser, and I met at a bar in Chinatown. They handed me the Asians' money in an envelope. I flew down to L.A., put in the order, and paid the Italians, who arranged for a truck to come up from L.A. with the goods. Nothing to it. Piece of cake.

Except somewhere between L.A. and San Francisco the truck disappeared. Or as I grudgingly realized, there never was a truck.

The Asians wanted their money back. Amy and especially Loser were shitting a building. Loser had visions of the Asians going Bruce Lee all over his ass. I flew back down to L.A. and set up a meeting with the Italian brothers at one of my bars. I made an impassioned and persuasive argument, emphasizing that I needed the Asians' money returned within twenty-four hours. The Italians were moved by my presentation and agreed. Unfortunately, I gave them twenty hours too long. The next morning the cops carted Italian Brother Number One off to jail and Italian Brother Number Two was discovered in the basement of a strip club with an ice pick in his neck.

The Asians expressed their condolences.

And they still wanted their money.

Around this time, my lawyer told me my court case was looking good. With a couple of breaks, I was almost sure to get probation. He suggested I move back to L.A. and show the court that I was cleaning up my act. The first thing I should do, my lawyer said, was get a respectable job.

So I went back to work at Felony Ford.

As soon as I settled back in L.A., Amy and Loser split San Francisco and moved to the Valley. Between my bar hustles and the shit I was pulling at Felony, I started sending the Asians regular payments. I felt I owed them. I was responsible for the busted deal and I wanted to pay them back, wanted to make it right. Once they saw that I was good for a small, weekly payment, they relaxed.

Then Loser showed up at my place one afternoon with a proposition. He said he had a way to clear the slate all at once. All I had to do was middle some cocaine for him. He knew the people I'd be moving between. They were stand-up guys, nothing like the Italians.

The deal smelled. I didn't want any part of it. It was just one deal, Amy said, and we'll be debt free, no more strings. It was tempting, I had to admit that.

I went for it and, of course, got fucked. Loser ended up ripping off everyone. The coke was bad and there was no money. We were burned and Loser was gone. He left Amy bawling on her couch and two big motherfuckers in my living room threatening to break my legs.

"I'm the middle man," I told one of them, the brains, the one with the third-grade education. "I got nothing out of this. I got beat, too."

"I don't give a shit about you," Brains said. "I want my fucking money."

"Listen carefully," I said. *"There is no fucking money!"*

"I don't care. I want it tomorrow!" Brains said. He named a bar I always went to. On his way out of my apartment, he put his foot through my television set.

Asshole. I had five more in the other bedroom.

Brains showed up at the bar the next night with his partner and two other tough guys.

I showed up with Charlie and two guys who were mobbed up and packing Uzis.

We all crowded around a back table. Charlie scratched the top of his head. He spoke very low and very slowly.

"You guys got beat. Oh well. Shit happens. Mark got beat, too. Now, you can let this die or we can settle it another way. Your choice."

I could see the veins in Brain's head bulging out as he weighed his options. It finally dawned on him: They'd just been offered a free pass. He nodded at his muscle. They got up and lumbered out of the bar. Meeting over.

I moved in with Charlie. The two of us were in constant play. We'd do our check splitting at banks, come home, count out our money, live large for a couple of days, then discover that we were both broke. Charlie put most of his money up his nose. I'd throw my cash around at all of my bars, buying drinks and dinner for anyone who looked vaguely familiar. Most of the time, though, I was buying groceries with bad checks because Charlie and I couldn't put twenty dollars together between us. He'd binge out on coke; I'd party hard on booze. In the end, we'd be sitting in the apartment, silently watching some dreary movie on TV, not saying a word, mutely planning our next move.

After a while, Charlie started running with a gang of stickup artists who were into some very heavy shit. These were professionals, guys who knew how to beat alarms and crack safes. They were into commercial heists, stuff you read about in the paper, the kind of stuff Hollywood dies for. One time Charlie heard about a place that was about to receive a shipment of gold from a postal truck. Charlie and his gang decided to rob the truck. He invited me in.

"That's too crazy for me," I said.

"We're talking big money," he said.

I shrugged. "Not my style."

"Yeah, I know. You'd rather schlep from bar to bar, nickel and diming yourself to death."

"You got a problem with my bar hustle?"

Charlie didn't say anything. He just kept on cutting lines of coke with a razor blade, his fingers chopping with the flourish of a sushi chef.

Charlie moved into his own place a few days after that. He and his gang pulled off the post office truck heist without a hitch. At least that's what the bar buzz said. Charlie never called me. Weeks went by, then months, and Charlie just dropped out of sight. I heard now and then that he was working with some deeply connected hitters and that he was doing a serious amount of freebasing. I ran into him a couple of times over the next few years, always in bars. He was constantly coked out of his mind and usually out of control. Once we got into a shouting match over some money I supposedly owed him. It was bullshit. If anything, Charlie owed me money. He suddenly screamed at me, shot out of his chair, and started swinging at me, wild, loopy left hooks that made him woozy and landed in the air. His eyes were red and wild. I kept my distance after that.

Between scams I worked a series of part-time jobs to bring in extra cash. Day labor stuff, nothing that lasted more than a few weeks. Probably my longest gig was painting cars for a crazy Lithuanian in a garage on a Van Nuys street corner. One night, I was drinking in some bar after work. My hands were streaked with metallic paint as I lifted my glass. The bartender came over and handed me the phone. It was Charlie. He said he needed to see me. I told him where I was, ordered another drink, lit a smoke, and waited.

About an hour later, Charlie shuffled into the bar. It had been a year or more since I'd seen him. He looked pale, and his eyes were burning and furious. His face was covered with stubble and his hair was matted. He looked like he hadn't slept in a week. He practically collapsed at my table. He grabbed my cigarettes and lit one. I ordered him a scotch.

"I know I was a shit," he said.

I shrugged.

We didn't say anything else for ten minutes. I let Charlie sit there and smoke and drink and get his bearings. He'd cough, then jerk his head to either side and rake his fingers through his hair. He seemed to drift away for minutes at a time. He'd called me for a reason. He would tell me the reason when he was ready.

"Me and these guys," Charlie said. He coughed again.

He mentioned two names. Guys I'd seen around. I knew they were mobbed up.

"They gave me five thousand dollars," Charlie said. "Five large. That's what they gave me. The going rate. Imagine that. The going rate is five grand."

He shook his head. He lit another cigarette, drained his drink, slammed the shot glass down on the table. I jumped.

"I didn't know . . .," Charlie said.

His voice trailed away.

"Didn't know what, Charlie?"

He looked at me. "I didn't know I would feel this way."

I wiped my face with the back of my hand. The smell of the dried paint across my knuckles jolted me. My eyes began to water. And then Charlie curled his shot glass into his chest, close to his heart, and held it there as if it were a tiny child he was protecting from harm.

"I didn't pull the trigger, Mark. I swear to God, I didn't."

He spoke slowly, deliberately, in a sad heavy tone, like a hymn. "I was the wheelman. I drove the car. My job was to get us out of there. That was my end. I knew it was a hit, they told me that. I knew what they were paying me for. I didn't know the guy. Frank Conrad. You know him? I don't think you do. He was an *unknown*. A character actor. A face in the crowd. Just a guy. Stole this guy's girl. That's what he did. This was over a woman."

He sniffed, then wiped his nose with his sleeve. "We waited for him. He pulled into his driveway. I drove up behind him. Boxed him in. Blasted the high beams. Doing my job. My end. I was the driver. That's it."

Charlie leaned forward and mouthed the next words so softly I almost had to read his lips. As he spoke, I felt as if this bar was a sanctuary and I was his confessor.

"It was easy, Mark. It was so easy. They got out and did it. It was fast. I saw the look on his face. I saw his *face*. Then I couldn't look anymore. I just drove out of there. Nobody spoke afterward. Not a word. It was done. This was over a woman."

Charlie reached across the table, and with eyes blazing, he grabbed my wrist and tore at my skin.

"I didn't shoot my gun," he hissed. "I did not shoot my gun."

He clenched at me. I bit my lip to fight the pain of his fingernails digging into my flesh. Finally Charlie released my wrist and slumped back into his chair.

"Mark," he said, "I'm not a killer."

Charlie stood up. His chair clattered to the floor behind him. He leaned both fists on the table. Then he reached over and rested a lump of a hand on my shoulder. I pressed my hand over his. Charlie stared at our two hands, mine on top of his. Our hands seemed far away, as though they belonged to two other men.

"I can't live with this," Charlie said.

He pulled his hand out from under mine, rubbed his fingers across his face, and walked out of the bar.

It would be twenty years before I would see Charlie again.

In 1979, with my court date a few months away, I got a call from Paul, my lawyer.

"I got a good feeling, Mark," he said. "Things go our way, we catch a couple breaks, the judge is having a good day, I'm seeing you walk away with probation."

"Lotta ifs there, Paul."

"Well, yeah, a few. You always have to throw luck in the equation."

"You can't bank on luck."

"I agree. Always better to make your own luck."

"What are you trying to say, Paul?"

"You need to make a good impression on the judge."

"Fine. I'll buy a new suit, I'll get a haircut, I'll take a shower. What do you want?"

He paused. "I want you to get married."

Now I paused. "I'm not sure I heard you right. These cheap plastic phones—"

"You heard me."

I paced across my living room, wandered in and out of rows of VCRs, loudspeakers, TV sets, and microwaves. My apartment was like a fucking Sears showroom.

"You think it'll help?"

"I know it will," Paul said. "If you get married, you'll show the court you're trying to change. It's a statement: You want to settle down, start a family, you want to start taking responsibility. Judges eat that shit up."

I pushed aside a bunch of crap on the couch and squeezed my ass between a microwave and a VCR. I rubbed my forehead.

"All right," I said. "I'll do it."

"You will?"

"Yeah. I'll get married."

"Mark . . . you'll need a woman."

"Don't worry," I said. "I got one."

Her name was Linda Lyons. She worked in the office at Felony Ford and we'd been seeing each other off and on for a few months. I'd found myself flirting with her when I came inside to close an order, then I found myself hanging around her desk longer than I realized. I liked Linda's honey-colored hair and her husky, sexy voice. And she had a shy smile. I liked that, too, and I liked how I could pretty much always make her laugh.

She had a daughter and a scrawny ex-husband who tried to act tough around her. She told me that one night they got into an argument and he hauled off and whacked her. That royally pissed me off. A couple of weeks after she told me that story, I happened to be at her place and the ex came in. He might've been drinking, I couldn't tell. I certainly was. He started to raise his voice, began shouting about child support, this and that, and he grabbed her arm. I went nuts. I shoved him up against the wall and jammed my fist into his throat.

"Listen, you little shit," I said. "This ain't my beef. You just don't touch her. You don't raise a finger to her. Because I'll fucking kill you."

That sealed it for her. I was her hero after that.

As for me . . .

I *thought* I loved her. Maybe. I don't know. My life was such a mess. I was feeling such heat. Between my court case and my cons, I was trying to keep so many balls in the air. I couldn't lose focus for even a second or all the balls would come crashing down. Linda didn't know a *tenth* of what was going on. I kept her out of it, kept her in the dark. I honestly thought that was the best way. She knew I had a court case. I told her that much. I couldn't tell her how deep into crime I was. I just couldn't tell her . . .

We got married in Vegas. My brother Stuart came along for the festivities. We sped through the desert, the three of us, blasting music in the car, my brother sprawled out on the backseat. I got us to the Strip in record time. I pulled into the first wedding chapel we could find. I barely remember the ceremony. I was drunk and Linda was giddy and my brother was itching to get to the casino. I slurred the words, "I do," puckered up to plant a kiss on Linda, staggered as a flashbulb went off in my face, and flinched as Stuart pelted me with a handful of rice. Linda wanted to spend a few days in Vegas, have a honeymoon like a normal newlywed couple. I couldn't afford the time. We spent one night, then hustled back, me at the wheel again, hands pressed into the steering wheel, eyes riveted on the road, foot to the floor.

The inside of the car was silent as a tomb.

All Linda wanted was to have a good marriage. She deserved that. She certainly did her part. She was loyal and fun and she hung in there, no matter what. She gave me the benefit of every doubt. As ridiculous as I was, she believed that I was doing the best that I could. I had so many distractions, though, that my best was pretty piss-poor.

At first we lived in her apartment. A couple of years later, Linda's father passed away and left her a trust fund. She used the money to buy a small house, something she'd always wanted. I always felt that it was her house, not mine. When I could, I helped out with the mortgage. Mainly, I did the upkeep. I liked to putter around, do minor repairs, mow the lawn, tend the garden. Believe me, I was no Mr. Fixit. I tried, though, gave it my best shot. If a pipe burst or something, I'd bang it with a hammer, see if I could pound it back into place. Who knows? Maybe I'd get lucky, save us a hundred bucks on a plumber. A couple of times I actually surprised myself and Linda. She found my home improvement skills funny. I can still hear her laughing while I was under the sink wrestling a pipe around, water and shit from the garbage disposal spraying all over the top of my head.

And then one day I fell in love.

Head over heels, stars in my eyes, unconditionally, crazy in love.

On September 5, 1980, my daughter, Heather, was born. The first time I saw her, I was gone. Over the moon. Weak-kneed. I still feel that way.

God, I love my daughter.

I spent as much time with Heather as I could. The morning, especially, that was our time. We'd make coffee, get bagels, and read the paper together. When she got a little older, I'd take her with me to Sunday morning swap meets. I'd work a booth and sell anything I could, some stuff I found, other stuff I bought with bad checks. Heather would sit on my lap and we'd sell together. I think she was the reason I made so much money at those swap meets. She was pretty irresistible. She looked like a mini-me. Chubby little face, red hair, blue eyes. And was she smart. You could show her something once and she'd pick it up. Especially math. That she got from my father. He had a fast, mathematical mind. I remember sitting around the dinner table with my family. My father would challenge all us kids with math problems. My brothers were hopeless. I was the only one who could keep up with him. He'd start easy, then try to stump me, and then I'd try to stump him. I couldn't do it. He had a head for figures, my dad. Yeah, he and my daughter both, fast, sharp minds . . .

6

The First Time

HEATHER

"My earliest, most vivid memory of my father was when I was two and a half, sitting in court. All this stuff was going on around me. I didn't understand what was happening. Didn't know what anything meant. Then I went home with my mom and he didn't."

Heather Borovitz sits huddled inside her leather jacket, waiting for the rain. Her hair is flame red, just like his used to be, her features round and soft, her forehead high, just like his. She taps out a cigarette from her pack, lights it, sips her coffee, absently spins her cell phone on the table before her. She laughs, a deep throaty laugh, a laugh hard and heavy with heartache.

"Check me out. Cigarettes, coffee, and a cell phone. I am totally my dad's daughter."

She speaks and something glistens from inside her mouth. A tongue ring.

"When I was a baby, I would only let him hold me. I would cry if anybody else even tried. One time, my uncle Stuart?—he passed away from MS—well, he looked like my father so he was holding me. My dad walked into the room and I realized my uncle was holding me and I started wailing. I mean, wailing. Yeah. I'd only let my dad hold me."

Heather tosses back her mane of wild red hair. "After that first time in prison, he promised me that he'd never go back. I believed him. He swore to me. I was only five or six. I remember that time so well. Sunday mornings we'd get up at 6 A.M. We'd get bagels, come home, make coffee, and I'd sit in his lap and read the newspaper with him. Then about six months later, I was sitting on the floor in my sister's room and my dad came in. He said the cops were looking for him again and he had to go away. It wasn't his fault, he told me. He was on the run, he said, and he'd come home when he could. He left. He came home every so often. He'd sneak in, bring us stuff, and then he'd disappear like some phantom. It was crazy. I was only five or six and he broke my heart."

A raindrop spatters her leather jacket. She doesn't notice or doesn't care. She crushes out her cigarette, lights another, drains her coffee.

"I couldn't tell my friends where my father was. It was too embarrassing. I was in Girl Scouts and we'd have these Father-Daughter things and I was the only one without a father. I'd make shit up. Then one time, for real, in the middle of the night, the SWAT team surrounded our house. Cops crashed into our house. They had shotguns, machine guns. It was frightening. Then even after they caught him, cops came to our house with guns drawn. My mother was like, 'You guys are so dumb. You already have him.' It was nuts. I didn't know he was so dangerous that they needed a SWAT team. Maybe it was because of the amount of money that was involved."

Heather tilts her head to the side, blows the smoke from her cigarette into the far end of the Starbucks parking lot.

"My dad and I went through a lot. I didn't talk to him for years. We've worked it through now. It wasn't easy. All those years when he was in prison, I always thought my dad was a

*good person. Didn't matter what he did. I believed in him.
I didn't care if he was the bad seed. No matter what, I always
thought my dad hung the moon. Yeah. I believed he hung the
moon."*

She smiles, a wide, defiant smile.

"I still do."

M y chest heaved as I waited for the judge to look up
from the sheaf of documents before him and deliver a
verdict. I shifted my weight. I became aware of a soft rustling
noise. I glanced over my left shoulder and I saw her.

Officer Schell.

She stood in the back of the courtroom, straight as a
knife, waiting, watching, her eyes creepy yellow beacons.

The judge sighed, peeked at me over his bifocals.

"Probation," he said.

My breath came out in a low whistle.

Behind me I heard the clop of footsteps and a distant door
slam.

Probation came with a catch: I had to pay back all the
money I'd stolen. To do that, I had to work out a payment
schedule with my probation officer. The PO asked for five
hundred dollars a month. I said, "Look, I'm between jobs
right now. I can't afford five hundred a month."

"Those are the terms. Five hundred a month. And you
have to pay every month, like clockwork. No exceptions."

"Fine," I said, and I paid him the first installment, with a
bad check.

I had to do it. I was afraid that if I didn't pay the five hundred right then, he'd send me to jail. And I gave him the bad

check knowing that I was going to cover it. I got in my car and headed straight to the bank. I just had to make one quick stop.

At my neighborhood tavern.

Hey, everybody, I got probation! We did it! It took years of extensions and negotiations and lawyering and getting married. In the end, it was all worth it. Let's have a toast. To probation!

Man, nothing better than sitting around a bar with my buddies, enjoying a little probation libation, celebrating my day in court before going over to the bank and making that check good. Okay, I'll have one more, Doc, and then I'm outta here. Ahhh. Hey, would you grill me up a burger, please? Make it a steak burger with fries. And another drink. Fuck it, make it a double, I'm in a good mood . . . in fact, one more round! For everybody! A round on me! To freedom!

Umm. Nobody makes a burger like you, Doc. No. Body. Umm ummm. Hey, hey, hey . . . where you going with that? Leave the bottle, Doc. It's a special occasion.

Better check the time. Don't want to miss getting over to the bank. Let's see, today's Friday. Banks close at six. Oh, got plenty of time. It's only . . .

Eight-thirty?

What the . . .?

That can't be right. It can't be eight-thirty. Doc, what time you got? Seriously? Shit. Cowboy, what does your watch say? Oh no! I'm fuckkked! What am I gonna do?

There is only one thing I can do.

Have another drink and worry about it on Monday.

No matter how hot I was, I always managed to keep one step ahead of the courts. I'd get busted, tossed into county jail, make bail, argue my case, plead hardship, and somehow convince the judge to give me a new trial date. I had so much shit pending, so many different counts against me, so many upcoming court dates, it was a nightmare keeping track. And as soon as I stepped out of county lockup, I was right back on the street, working some scam, and writing a rubber check.

In March 1984, the screws tightened. I knew I was running out of time. I prepared a deal. I went before a judge in superior court and presented a proposal.

"Your Honor," I said, "I know we've been talking about a two-year deal."

The judge studied me for a moment before he spoke. He was a stocky man with an egg-shaped head and a bushy white mustache. He looked more like a dockworker than a judge.

"Mr. Borovitz," the judge said, "do you know how many times you have been in front of my court? I've lost count. Two years is not enough for what you've done."

"Your Honor, I want to make restitution to the people I've harmed. I want to pay them back. I can't do that if I go to prison."

"How do you propose to make restitution? Where are you going to get the money?"

"My wife and I have discussed this. We're willing to take out a second mortgage on her house. If you send me to prison and I take out a second, the bank will foreclose on the house. I'm proposing probation so I can pay them back."

The judge pressed his fingers against his forehead. He was thinking about my deal. I studied his eyes. He was wavering in my direction. I could see it. I had him.

"Your Honor, may I approach?"

I looked up and there she was . . . Officer Schell, walking toward the bench. She was wearing a simple black dress. She looked as if she were going to a funeral. She ignored me and handed the judge a stack of checks two inches thick.

"Your Honor, these are bad checks this gentleman has written . . . *since he was last let out of jail.*"

My lawyer leaned over to me. He spoke in a frantic stage whisper. "Agree to three years."

"I heard that," the judge said. "Mr. Borovitz, I'd take your lawyer's advice."

"Three years in state prison?"

"Take it," my lawyer said.

I swallowed. "Okay. I'll take the three years."

I glanced at Officer Schell. Her face was expressionless, a mask of stone. She began flattening the front of her dress with her palm, over and over, as if she were brushing crumbs off her lap. She abruptly dropped her hands to her side and assumed a military position, her back ramrod straight. We locked eyes.

And she winked at me.

C hino State Prison sits in the middle of flatland, a good half a mile from the main road. It stares at the highway, a grim, nondescript concrete cluster. Only as you get closer do you see the guard towers patrolled by machine gunners and the barbed wire looped around the circumference like a jagged metal ribbon.

The bus we called the Gray Goose chugged past the front of the prison and crunched slowly up a gravel road to the back of the complex. The bus crawled toward a mammoth, rusted iron gate. The gate swung slowly open, creaking like the door to a haunted castle. The bus idled as the gate heaved and moaned and then lurched to a stop. Then the bus drove onto the prison grounds and the gate clanged shut behind us.

A cold jolt ran through me. Suddenly I had no idea what to do. I had no idea how I was going to live. I was lost. I was utterly and totally lost. I shivered uncontrollably.

And then I began to retch.

I was put into a ten-foot-square cell. I was not alone. My cellmate, a tall, bug-eyed mute who furiously scratched his tangled mess of stringy brown hair with both hands as if he had lice, sat crouched in the corner. I rolled onto a narrow, stained cot across the cell from him. We didn't speak. He stared and I stared back.

"How you doing, Professor," I mumbled.

He grunted and raked his fingernails through his scalp.

Misery, black and cold, descended on me like a curtain. My head throbbed with fever, my stomach ached, and my body shook. I spent my first three days in prison in a fetal position, immobile, lying on my threadbare cot with the matzo-thin mattress, detaching myself from drink and keeping an eye on the Professor. We never spoke. On day four, a guard escorted him out of the cell, transferring him, no doubt, to the wacko ward. The next day my fever broke. The shakes subsided to occasional trembling. I was able to sit up and eat and smoke.

A week later I was moved to Reception Yard Central, a purgatory where I was forced to wait another three weeks to get my final assignment. I feared that I would be transferred out of Chino, into another facility somewhere else in the state.

I desperately wanted to stay so that Linda and Heather could visit me on weekends. The decision was out of my hands. I could only wait.

Finally, I got the word: Reception Yard West. I was relieved. RYW was a Level Two yard, a lower-security yard. We were pretty much allowed the run of the outside, which included a wide-open expanse with a walking area and a few picnic tables. At night we slept in double bunks in a Quonset hut, a large room that held about 150 men. It felt like a military barracks, except we were prisoners, not soldiers, and our uniforms were orange jumpsuits.

In the beginning I kept to myself. I was determined to stick by all the rules. I didn't want trouble from inmates or guards. In my mind, the system had beaten me once. I would do my time like a model prisoner, maybe get out early for good behavior, then hit the streets and pick up my hustle. Next time, though, I'd be more careful. I'd keep my eyes open. You can't trust anybody. Half the people are idiots, the other half are out to fuck you. Linda was one of the few good ones. I could trust her.

And Heather . . . I had to make this up to her. I had made a promise that I wouldn't go away. I wanted to get out of prison so I could spend more time with her. Keep my promises. She was only a kid. Yes, I had to get out for Heather. She needed her dad.

A week after I got assigned to Reception Yard West, a guy came to see me.

"Borovitz, huh? You Jewish?"

"Yeah. Got a problem with that?"

I had put on a ton of weight at this time. I tipped the scale at well over three hundred pounds. I had shaved my head and I looked menacing. This guy was puny and nervous and I towered over him.

"No, no, I'm Jewish, too. That's why I came over. I'm Sheldon."

Sheldon had an annoying high-pitched whine of a voice. He was the nerdy kid who always got beat up at school.

"I figured you were Jewish. I like to look out for the Jewish inmates."

I winced. Shit. If he's looking out for us Jews in here, we got trouble.

"Sheldon, huh?" I said.

"Yeah. Or Shel, if you prefer. Shelley is okay, too. My friends call me Shelley."

He flicked at an invisible speck of dirt that had dropped onto his sleeve. He shifted his weight back and forth, as if he had to take a serious piss.

"Mark," I said, and we shook hands.

"I figure we should stick together," Sheldon said.

"A lot of people stick with their own in here. I noticed that," I said.

"Oh yeah," Sheldon said. "Stay away from the AB. Aryan Brotherhood. They slit a black guy's throat the other day. And I heard the Mexican Mafia tossed a guy off the third tier over at Central."

"You're a walking newscast."

"Information is power," Sheldon said.

I smiled. Sheldon was growing on me.

"The best way to get through this is to get a job. I can help you with that."

"Thanks. I'm telling you, Shelley, I'm going nuts with boredom."

Sheldon grinned, exposing a panel of teeth the color of scrambled eggs.

"The prisoners run everything around here," he said. "Those of us who work get the best treatment. Work is the key to the whole deal."

Then Sheldon lowered his voice as if he were about to give me directions to the hideout. "You start out doing temp work in the hope that your job will pan out and you'll stick. Things go right, you get lucky, they'll put you in PWC."

"PWC?"

"Permanent work crew. You get to move into the PWC dorm, which is half the number of inmates, your own single bunk, TV privileges. And in PWC, you get better food. Bagels, hamburgers . . . not that the food here is *bad* . . ."

Sheldon winked at me and smiled. We both started to laugh. Over time I would learn that Sheldon London was a notorious embezzler, adept at insurance fraud and money laundering, and that he had a black belt in karate.

"Can you type?" Shelley asked me.

"Sure," I said. "I'm an excellent typist."

"Okay, so you can't type."

"What gave me away?"

"Your eyes. You looked down for half a second. It's a tell. Work on that."

"Okay, I will." I rocked back on my heels, and Shelley London and I laughed again.

"I'll learn to type," I said.

"Rabbi Silverman needs a clerk. You work with him sometimes and as an assignment clerk other times. It's all typing."

"I don't have to take a test, do I?"

Shelley London gave my shoulder a little tap. "You just did, Big Guy."

MEL

His hair is all white now, snowcap-mountain white, and his neatly trimmed, frosty beard hides two dimples. He has an athlete's build still, powerful arms and shoulders; he has played some ball. His voice is clean and curious, its tone melodic, a soft baritone. His blue eyes twinkle.

"I tell you, he just has to put up his pinky and he's got you."

The grin bubbles into a small laugh.

"He is a very convincing guy. It used to make me think of that word. Convincing. Con right up front."

Rabbi Mel Silverman leans back into the overstuffed armchair in his modest living room.

"The first time Mark came in, he showed no potential for transformation of any kind. He came in like a mainline inmate. Brazen. Cocky. I didn't see much inclination that he would change his way of life. Too torn inside. Going too many ways. He was just full of energy and intelligence. Smarts.

"We had a few talks. I asked him, 'You've got so many abilities, why are you using them for this stuff?' He didn't really want to deal with it. His only concern was his family—his wife, his stepdaughter, and his daughter. Heather. She was maybe four or five. Flaming red hair. A little replica of her father."

Mel smiles. "The first time, his biggest drive was to have enough to eat. It was mainly about food. We had a refrigerator. We would get donations for the holidays, bagels for after services, sometimes a challah, like that. When Mark became my clerk, I put him in charge of the refrigerator. He seemed like a natural. And he was. He took that job seriously. Yeah, first time in, Mark was keeper of the food."

Mel Silverman folds his hands in his lap.

"He wasn't interested in changing his way of life. He was more interested in angles. How to run his game, how to get more cigarettes, how to beat the other inmates. He was a gambler. Prison became almost an extension of his street life. It was virgin territory for his cons.

"Mark was an early bird. He got up before everyone else. He was heavy, he smoked, and yet he had some sense of trying to take care of himself. Every morning he'd take a mile walk around the track. I don't know. Maybe it wasn't for his health. Maybe it was just a time for him to regroup, figure out his day. Then he'd come in and start his work."

Rabbi Silverman stands and disappears into his galley kitchen for a moment, returns holding a can of diet Dr Pepper. He settles back into his chair.

"He was a hustler, a man mastered by his appetites. He had some pangs of guilt about his family. Some. He was confused about direction. As a clerk, he used to play the angles afforded him. For example, he'd organize pizza sales to benefit the chapel. That first time, I don't think he cared much about the chapel. He cared about the pizzas. So he'd work hard, get all the guys involved. He took his job seriously. One time, Shelley London put a sandwich into the refrigerator. It was for later, for lunch. Mark was in charge of that fridge. He felt responsible for it. So Mark's out doing something and this other inmate, big guy from New York, guy called the Brick, took out Shelley's sandwich and started eating it."

Mel chuckles. "I'll never forget it. There's the Brick munching away at the sandwich and Mark comes in. Mark goes crazy. Nuts. He snaps. He charges into Brick like a ram, butts him in the stomach. The sandwich goes flying. Mark grabs this big guy by the throat, and he turns beet red.

He starts screaming, 'You touch my refrigerator again, I'll kill you!'

"Oh yeah. That first time? It was all about food."

I moved into the PWC dorm. We were the privileged few, eighty cons, defined by our single beds and our prison jobs. For a lot of guys, this was a major upgrade from the life they had been leading. They had three hots and a cot. They were off the street, off drink, off drugs, and relatively safe, although you had to watch your back at all times. We had a TV and if you had half a brain, some card sense, or a decent sports opinion, you could be flush with smokes or even cash. As for me, I was *rich*.

It started with baseball. I've always loved baseball. It's by far the best game for bettors. You don't have to deal with point spreads. All you have to do is pick the winner. Well, you have to give odds. That's okay. You need some challenge.

Those of us who liked baseball began betting the games every day. As soon as we'd go to our jobs, we'd call each other and get our bets down. It was kind of funny. There I was using the prison telephone to make a Red Sox–Indians parlay. Parlays paid a big return: one carton of cigarettes to make three. In addition to making bets, I was booking bets. The bets and the butts started rolling in. It was Vegas in Chino.

I got set up as assignment clerk, which was a pretty powerful position. If somebody wanted a job or wanted to change jobs, they had to go through me. It cost 'em. Depending on the assignment, the price could go as high as three cartons of cigarettes. Then at night, we'd play cards. Those marathon gin games with my family paid off. I kicked ass. I was dorm champion. Summer passed and football season and the baseball

playoffs started. It was 1984 and the Cubs were playing the
Padres. I loved the Cubs. Bet a shitload on them. They lost.
Cost me ten cartons of cigarettes. Thankfully football moved
into full swing and I teamed up with another guy. He was Professor College; I was Dr. Pro. By the Super Bowl, I had made
back all the cartons I'd lost.

I also made smokes and money typing. Guards would
come into the clerk's office and ask me to type their reports
and letters. It was appalling how illiterate they were. Forget
about writing a letter. They couldn't put together a sentence.
I'd correct the spelling, fix up the grammar. Half the time I'd
write the whole letter. I started to get a reputation for being
the smart guy, the Brain. Inmates would show up at the office
or see me in the yard and ask me to type their appeals. I estab-
lished a fee for that: five cartons of cigs. Then some of them
asked me to *write* their appeals. I charged them ten cartons for
that and ten more cartons if they won.

During that first stay, Linda and Heather managed to visit
me almost every weekend. Like clockwork, every Sunday, I'd
have lunch in the yard with my family. I can only imagine what
went through Linda's mind as she loaded up the car. I mean,
what a way to spend every Sunday—driving out to the middle
of the moon to visit Daddy in the strange, cold, concrete village
behind the barbed wire fence. I'm sure Linda and Heather were
hassled by the guards. I'm certain the guards searched them
and interrogated them and rummaged through their picnic bas-
ket looking for a weapon or a bottle or a serrated-edged spoon
that I could use to dig myself out *Shawshank Redemption*
style. I admired Linda's strength, determination, loyalty, and,
especially, her great spirit. I admired her and I was thankful to
her because she was all that I had.

Heather and I would play games in the yard. When the

brutal afternoon sun started beating down, we'd find a shady spot and we'd go over her schoolwork. She was only in kindergarten so there wasn't too much to go over. I started pushing her ahead, teaching her the multiplication tables just for fun. We made it a game, used a deck of cards. She picked the tables right up. She was a natural, just like her grandfather. Had the potential to be a famous mathematician or successful bookmaker.

"Are you sure you don't know these already?" I asked her.

"Nope."

"Are you conning me?"

"*Nooo.*"

"Because it's okay if you are. I wouldn't mind."

"The first time I learned this was today."

"So if you're not conning me, you know what you are?"

"What?"

"*Smart!*"

And I grabbed her and tickled her and she shrieked, "*Daddy! Stop!*"

And we both laughed and laughed . . . until we cried.

In memory, the moments blur. Some moments I've tucked away on purpose and some I've simply forgotten. That's what happens when time is repeated, day after day, hour after hour, minute by minute. In prison you are on a treadmill, walking, walking, walking . . . and going nowhere.

At Chino, it was all about the morning. Every morning was exactly like the morning before. It became about how you faced the day. How you took on that morning. How you made something of your waking hours. In other words, how you made something out of nothing.

Every morning I walked at dawn. The sour stench of cow shit from a nearby farm drifted over the yard like a cloud and caused my nose to crinkle up. The stink was my morning walking partner. It shook me awake like a slap across the face. I'd sometimes see another lone inmate taking the same walk.

"Nothing like the smell of fresh cow shit in the morning!" I'd say. I'd spread my arms wide and pretend to fill up my lungs with a gulp of fresh air. I'd get either a laugh or a look.

And at Chino, it was all about the night. The night was black, black as oblivion, black as a void. With the blackness came the sounds of hell: howls of suffering, of pain, of loss, of loneliness, of anger, of fear, of desperation, of longing, of hatred, of sex; voices of men talking, laughing, arguing, crying, swearing, screaming, moaning, singing, rapping, praying; violent scratching, tapping, scraping, pounding, clanging, beating.

Oh yeah. Hell is a prison night.

Mel tried to talk to me. At first he was casual, then as my release date got closer, he got more insistent. He tried to get through to me. I listened respectfully, which meant I wasn't listening at all. I certainly wasn't *hearing*. We talked a little bit about the Torah. I always turned it around, got Mel to tell some stories, to have some fun. I didn't take him seriously. He was a nice guy, and I knew he believed what he said and it was good for some people. I just wasn't one of them.

I was a criminal. I had an image to protect. In many people's eyes, including Mel's, I was a powerful figure. A bigger-than-life Jewish gangster. Mel was preaching a whole other way, a path that was fine for other people. This path had nothing to do with me. He wanted me to quit the Life. He wanted me to turn my back on my own image.

He wanted me to be *ordinary*.

I could not do that. I had to be bigger, larger. I had to live in the fantasy of the crime world because in that world, I was important. It didn't matter what that world was. It only mattered that in that world, I was *somebody*.

7

The Last Time

MEL

"Life's curveballs," says Rabbi Mel Silverman. "I am always intrigued by those moments, events that, at the time they occur, appear to be accidents. Luck. Mark, of course, calls these accidents God. I don't know. As I get older, I find myself seeing so many ways of God, the possibilities of God intruding. I persist in questioning, even if it brings me discomfort. I find I don't mind the discomfort. Because for me, theologically, it's more important to have truth than comfort."

Mel caresses his neatly trimmed white lawn of a beard. "I became a prison chaplain quite by accident. Apparent accident. I had been a traditional congregational rabbi. It wasn't really me. It wasn't my calling. It didn't give me enough room to be the rabbi I wanted to be. I wanted to do more teaching, especially in small groups. I prefer that kind of intimacy. I'm more of a one-on-one rabbi.

"I was taking a Talmud class at Hebrew Union College in L.A. One of the other rabbis in the class was an Orthodox rabbi named Izzy Cutler. Like many Orthodox families, Izzy had a lot of children. He was very concerned about his financial survival. He had taken a job as a prison chaplain to make extra money. Right before Passover, he comes into class with a long face.

" 'Things okay, Izzy?' I ask him.

"He says, 'Mel, I'm miserable. I got fired.'

" 'What happened?'

" 'I wanted to have a seder at the prison,' Izzy says, 'so I brought in a couple of gallons of Manischevitz wine. I carried them into the kitchen. I gave them to a couple of workers in white uniforms and hats. I assumed they were staff.'

" 'I'm preparing for Passover,' I tell them. 'Put these in a safe place, away from the inmates.' "

Mel interrupts himself with a abrupt laugh. "Well, of course, they were inmates. PWC. Just like Mark. About three hours later, there's a free-for-all in the mess hall and kitchen. Guys are drunk, fighting, bloodied up. Security comes running in, whistles blowing, batons waving, and in the middle of it all are the empty gallon bottles of Manischevitz wine."

" 'I got canned,' Izzy says. 'I don't know what I was thinking. I feel like I left my inmates in a lurch. Why don't you apply for the job, Mel? I really want to know if my inmates are all right.'

"So I did. The timing was perfect. I had just left my temple in Newport Beach. Before I became a rabbi, I'd worked at juvie, Juvenile Hall in East L.A. and South L.A., as a probation counselor. I figured these were just adult juveniles. I was pretty much right. I got the job and I stayed for twenty-five years."

Mel Silverman shrugs and allows himself a final ironic chuckle.

"Maybe Mark is right," he says. "Maybe there are no accidents. Maybe those accidents are God."

I circled my release date on my calendar and I counted the days. Actually, I counted the *hours*. To me, it was like a countdown at the start of a New Year. As the days got closer to my release date, my body started to tingle in anticipation. I was like a switch, ready to ignite the power.

They drove us out of Chino in a rickety van with a bad muffler. We bumped along the back road, out onto the highway, away from the nation of concrete gray into a world of Technicolor. Everything looked bright and new. The sky was as blue as a postcard, and the air smelled of freshly mowed grass. I closed my eyes and sighed. *Eighteen months in lockup.* Bouncing along in that piece of shit van, heading out of Chino on my car ride to freedom, I never felt more alive. I basked in the word itself, let it flow over me like a hot shower: *release.*

To be set free.

And then my mind flipped to the back of the word, and I dropped the *re* and focused on *lease,* and I saw that *lease* was just another word for *rent,* as in *how* to pay the *fucking rent* and my momentary rush of freedom was zapped and replaced by a sudden and vicious stab of anxiety that tore through me, and as the van drove onto the *free*way, to take me home, I started to tremble.

I was free and I wasn't. I was different and I was the same. I wanted to be a better father and husband, and I still wanted to be the same happy-go-lucky fun guy. When I moved back in with Linda and Heather, I came on too strong. Linda was tense around me, cold at times. Who could blame her? I had shaken her world. Hell, I'd picked up her world and turned it over. She didn't know who I was. She'd spent so much time adjusting to my absence that having me around jarred her even more. I didn't know what to say half the time. I was not saying enough, or I was saying too much or I was saying the wrong thing. And I was freaking out about our finances. I would say that we had hit bottom, except that bottom would've been a whole flight up.

And then there was Heather. My first or second day out, a Friday, I sat with her on the floor of her room and told her that I would never go back to prison again. She threw her arms around my neck and held me and wouldn't let go.

"Promise me, Daddy."

"I promise," I said. "I'll never go back."

The rest of the weekend, she wouldn't leave my side. We did everything together. Hung out, watched TV, read the paper, cooked eggs, toasted bagels. Monday morning, I took her to school. We stuck together in the playground. When the bell rang and it was time to line up to go inside, she refused. She grabbed me and clung to me.

"You gotta go to school, honey," I said.

"No," Heather said.

"Come on. You gotta go. It's the *law*."

"I'm not going."

"Heather—"

She was getting desperate. "Please, Daddy."

She started to sniffle, then she started to cry. I picked her up and carried her into her classroom. She was wailing. I tried to reason with her. There was no consoling her. I handed my daughter to her teacher, who pulled her out of my arms. My eyes filled with tears as I watched my daughter scream. Her only thought was that I was abandoning her.

"Daddy! No! Don't leave me, Daddy! *DON'T LEAVE ME!*"

I wanted to cover my ears to block out her cries. Then I wanted to charge back into that classroom and carry Heather— my companion, my pal, my partner—out into my world.

Instead, I turned my back on her and walked away.

From October 1985 until December 16, 1986, I lived a life that was careening out of control. Remember the movie *Speed*, about the bus that had to stay above fifty-five miles per hour at all times or it would blow up? That was me. I was the bus.

The question, of course, is *why*? Why didn't I choose to start a new life? Maybe my family life wasn't the way I idealized it when I was staring at the cracked and peeling ceiling in the slam. Of course, I'd conveniently forgotten that I'd gotten married for a dubious reason, to keep myself out of jail. Love? What's love got to do with it? Linda and I certainly had good times. Those times and the couple we used to be seemed like a photograph from someone else's life. When we were together there was tension, and often shouting, much of it by me. Mostly, there was silence. Much of it from me.

I was happy when I was with Heather. I wanted to give her the world. No, that's not right. I wanted to *buy* her the world. One glitch. I didn't have any money. I vowed to get money, to score, and score big.

They say that prison time scares some people straight. Prison didn't scare me at all. Chino was Camp Snoopy. If you were smart and could work your game, it was easy time. When I got out, I had no fear of breaking my parole, of getting caught, or of going back in. I thought I was smarter than the cops. I had to work fast and furious to make up for lost time.

I went back to cars. I threw in with a guy named Bunner who had a simple, solid hustle going. We'd buy cars, roll back the miles, then sell these lemons to dealers. It was fast and clean because I'd just write a bad check for the car. Oh yeah. I was still writing trash. How soon did I start? The moment

I stepped out of the prison van. I didn't hit the ground running; I hit the ground *writing*.

The problem with this hustle was that Bunner turned out to be a piece of shit. One day a dealer called him. He was pissed off. He'd discovered that a car we'd sold him had a dirty odometer. Bunner said he was shocked and dumped the whole scam in my lap. Just nailed me. Fucked me over.

I confronted him in a restaurant. I got up in his face and started shouting. The manager came over and asked us to leave. We went out into the parking lot and got into his car. One of Bunner's pals was riding shotgun. I got into the back.

We drove off. Bunner started accusing me of stealing from him. Congratulations, I told him, you finally figured it out. I'd been stealing from him because he'd been stealing from me. We stopped at a red light, and Bunner turned around and threw a punch at me. I slipped it and clocked him in the jaw. Bunner's head shot back, bouncing off the steering wheel. He came back at me and tried another weak punch, which missed me by a mile. I snapped a jab off his nose and got out of the car. Bunner sped away.

"Go fuck yourself!" I screamed after him. I picked up a rock from the road and threw it in the direction of the fleeing car's taillights. I looked around to get my bearings. Fortunately, I wasn't far from a bar I knew. I ducked in there for the rest of the night to regroup.

The state got in touch with me. They sent a letter saying they wanted to see me. They had reason to believe I was rolling back odometers and writing bad checks. I burned the letter with my cigarette lighter.

Within a month, I had half a dozen bank accounts working at different banks. I kept the car scam going myself, buying high milers with bad checks, flipping back the miles, selling the cars, and cashing good checks, hoping to make the bad checks good and turning a profit. It was a speed hustle and I never really kept track of all the transactions. I was drinking too much to focus on details.

I knew the heat was on so I split from the house. I checked in with my parole officer weekly, like I was supposed to. Somehow I always missed him. Guess I called him when he was out or on the other line. We just never managed to connect. Oh well.

Linda was beside herself with worry and rage. The cops were hounding her on the phone, showing up at her door, looking for me. She told them she didn't know where I was, which was the truth. I was on the run, living in fleabag motels, on friend's couches, in the Cowboy's trailer. I'd go for days without getting in touch with Linda, then I'd sneak into her house and leave her money or food. I'd fill up the fridge with ice cream for Heather and steaks for her, then I'd disappear into the night. I was like a Jewish Zorro.

Sometimes I met them in safe spots. Restaurants, a park, places where I could hang out with Heather for a little while. She had no idea what was going on.

"When are you coming home, Daddy?"

"Soon, baby, soon," I'd lie.

I couldn't look her in the eye. She was so innocent, so trusting of me. And I'd made that promise.

And Linda? Well, Linda was just disgusted with me.

I wanted so badly to be with them. And I wanted so much to run away. I wanted to hide. I wanted to end this insanity. I wanted . . .

God knows. I was fucking lost. I was burning up. On fire. I was a stick of dynamite burning at both ends, watching myself about to blow up.

And I was drinking. Jesus, was I drinking. I was up to a gallon of whiskey a day. I drank all day and all night. My hand was always around a glass or a bottle. I was constantly hammered. I don't know how I got through the day. Don't know how I had enough strength or energy to live my life. Couldn't tell you how I found my way to my bed for the night.

Pedal to the metal. Drive. Don't let up. Don't slow down. Faster. If you go fast, they can't catch you.

It didn't occur to me that you could also crash.

I sat down with a pad and pencil and I crunched some numbers. I calculated that, more or less, I'd written between fifty thousand and seventy-five thousand dollars in bad checks. It suddenly struck me how I could get straight in one day. It was so simple that I was shocked I hadn't thought of it before.

I'd go to Vegas and get it all back betting football.

All I had to do was bet a ten-team teaser at 350 to 1. If I wagered three hundred bucks, I'd make close to a hundred thousand dollars. I'd pay the taxes and come home with enough money left to pay off the checks and split the rest with Heather and Linda.

This was a no-brainer, especially because I was going to bet a ten-team *teaser,* which meant I got an extra six points in every game to move the betting line any way I pleased. So if I liked a team that was favored by seven points, in the teaser I'd adjust the line my way, making it favored by only one! Of course, I had to win all ten games. No big deal. I was hot and when you're hot, you press up.

It was Thursday, December 16, 1986, two-thirty in the afternoon. I was living on a pullout cot in a friend's trailer. The place stank of cat piss. I spent as little time there as possible, using the trailer only to shower and sleep it off.

I polished off a burger and a couple of belts at a bar on Ventura Boulevard, then popped into a 7-Eleven near the corner of Van Nuys and Fulton. I picked up the *Los Angeles Herald-Examiner*, the gambler's newspaper of choice. I pulled out the sports section, perused Allan Malamud's column, ripped out the pro football lines, and started circling my picks in pen right on the page.

I didn't even think about my selections. I was in some kind of zone. It was as if there was a force coursing through me, making the picks for me. My hand flew down the page, whipping little circles around each winner. My hand felt light as air and I kept circling, circling, circling . . . the first game, second, third . . . all the way through number ten . . .

I approached the street corner. Somewhere in the back of my mind, I sensed that the light had switched from red to green. I didn't see it. I *sensed* it, as if I was blind. I stepped off the curb and started to cross the street. I never looked up from the paper.

As I walked across the street at Van Nuys and Fulton, the letters and numbers on the page suddenly seemed to get bigger, bolder. The letters were *huge*. I blinked. I had to be drunk. I kept walking. My legs felt heavy. It was as though I was walking in slow motion.

"Mark?"

At the sound of my name, a light flashed. *Woom!* Like a flashbulb going off in my eyes. I looked up. The light hung there for a moment, like an aura. And then it faded.

"Mark."

A white Ford Fairmont had pulled over at the corner of

Fulton and Victory. Its crimson hazard lights flashed in a rhythm, wham *wham,* like a heartbeat. The car was ten feet away.

"Over here."

I hadn't seen the car stop. I hadn't seen anything except the pro football games on the page of the *Herald* and the flash of light in my eyes. I don't remember walking over to the car. Suddenly, though, I was standing on the sidewalk, leaning into the passenger's window, staring at the passenger's face. I didn't recognize him. I knew, though, that he was a cop.

"Mark Borovitz, right?"

"Yeah." I could've denied it. I just didn't. I didn't think. I couldn't think. My head began to throb. "Is there a problem, Officer? I was crossing with the green—"

"I think I saw a wanted poster on you up in Santa Barbara."

"Me? That's impossible. I'm a law-abiding citizen."

"Pretty sure it was you."

"I get that a lot. I have one of those faces. I look like everybody's cousin. Sorry. I'm afraid you made a mistake."

My head was pounding. I grimaced. Tried not to let the pain show. A pond of sweat formed on my forehead. I swiped at it with the back of my hand. The cop looked me over. He was typical plainclothes LAPD, thick neck, wraparound Dirty Harry shades, movie star haircut.

"You all right?"

"I'm fine."

I don't know what I was. I was hot and I was cold and I was calm. Weirdly calm.

"Tell you what, Mark. Let's take a drive over to the Van Nuys police station. It's five minutes away. We'll check it out. If it's a mistake, we'll let you go. No harm, no foul."

At the word *we,* I got a chill. I had forgotten about the

driver. Suddenly, my body started to sag, to deflate. I felt as if the air had been let out of me, while at the same time something enormous was pressing down on my shoulder with immense strength, like a giant hand, and I thought that I was going to be smashed into the sidewalk, crushed into a mound of sand.

"It's a mistake," I mumbled. I spoke so softly and so feebly that I could barely hear my own voice.

And then the driver leaned over so I could see her face. She grinned, a tight, hard, triumphant grin, and my eyes fastened into her tiny yellow eye dots and my chill turned hot, white-hot, and I thought my cheeks would burst into flame.

"Hello, Mark," said Officer Schell.

The Dirty Harry cop slipped icy handcuffs over my wrists and shoved me into the backseat. Two helicopters whirred and fluttered overhead.

"SWAT," Officer Schell said. "Probably looking for you, Mark."

She pulled into traffic. I said nothing. She drifted into the left lane, then whipped into a U-turn in the middle of the street. My stomach lurched.

I pushed back against the seat and studied my hands, clasped together by the handcuffs. Except for my one mangled finger, I had graceful hands, the hands of a pianist or pickpocket. These hands had dug deep into car engines to turn back the truth. These hands had written thousands of dollars of bad checks, drained bank accounts, ruined lives. And these hands had held my daughter close to my heart. I wondered when I would do that again.

I knew then that I had to find another purpose for these hands. I knew that I had to stop this life. Had to. I knew that

I had a purpose other than this, and that I had to find out what it was, or I would die. It was that simple. That clear. That real.

And I knew that I had no choice. That I was being led. I knew it. This was perhaps the most stunning shock of all.

I believe that we have a choice. I believe that people are driven by free will. I believe it with all my heart. We have *a choice*.

And I believe with all my heart that at that moment, riding in the backseat of that car, starting when I crossed the street at Fulton at Van Nuys, that I had no choice. This was my Red Sea. This was my miracle.

I shivered because I knew what was happening. I knew I was about to commit myself to a different life, a changed life, and that it was going to take time and that it was going to be hard, and that I would be tempted a thousand times to turn back, to run away. I knew I was in for a fight. A fight against my inclinations, my tendencies, my temptations. A fight against myself. The fight of my life. The fight *for* my life.

And I knew that when I heard the voice call out "Mark?" that it wasn't the voice of the cop. I knew it was the voice of God.

I pulled my hands toward my face and felt tears running down my cheeks. Soft, warm, quiet tears.

The piece of newspaper from the *Herald* crinkled in my pocket.

After the cops booked me, they put me in a holding cell and let me have one phone call. I called Linda. I hadn't spoken to her in a nearly a week.

"Linda," I said, "I'm in jail."

She couldn't disguise the relief in her voice. "At least

you're alive." Then she got pissed. "Did you know the SWAT team was here? The cops come here every day looking for you, like you're Public Enemy Number One."

I chuckled.

"Oh, you think it's funny? Heather is scared to *death*—"

"I'm sorry, Linda, I didn't mean—"

"You're always sorry, Mark, and you never mean it."

I gripped the phone and waited. The silence tore at me. Finally, Linda sighed. "Okay. Let's get this moving. Which bondsman do you want me to call?"

I switched the phone to my other ear. My voice cracked. "I don't want you to call anybody."

"What?"

"Don't call anyone. The man upstairs is trying to tell me something. I have to sit here until I figure out what it is."

"You don't want to post bond?"

"No. It's different now. I can't say how. It's just different."

"Mark—"

"Linda, please, I have to figure this out." I spoke with such passion that Linda just sighed. I said, "I really am sorry this time. I really am."

She sniffed. "Okay."

"Please tell Heather that I love her. That's all I ask."

"I will."

Then I took a deep breath. "Good-bye, Linda."

"Good-bye, Mark," she said.

The circus started after that. I got sick, brutally sick. Shakes, hallucinations, vomiting. Textbook DTs. I woke up in the hospital ward. I guess the doctors started to worry because they called Linda. She checked in every five minutes to make sure I wasn't dying. She got through to me once, and I calmed her down. And then I drifted off to sleep . . .

My bed in the hospital ward is freezing and wet, and I am soaked in a river of my own sweat. My body convulses. My lips are dry and caked. My eyes bulge open. I follow a cockroach's climb up the wall in front of me. I am stuck to the mangy mattress pad, my senses assaulted with men's screams and the persistent stench of puke and urine. I cannot move. I dare not move. My eyes descend and I dream.

I am in a desert. It is unbearably hot. Sand engulfs me, swirling around me like a private tornado. Little storms pelt my eyes, ears, nostrils, and mouth. I spit out a mouthful of sand.

A shadowy figure walks toward me. It is a man. His body ripples with taut muscle. I don't know him. Something about him, though, is familiar. I've seen him before. I strain to remember where. I can't. And then his face morphs into my father's and I gasp. And then he is my brother Stuart and he begins to cough. And then he is Mario. Finally, he is someone I've never seen before, a stranger. And then he has no face at all.

We start to wrestle. He's strong and slippery and I can't get a grip on him anywhere. I dive for his legs, come up with another mouthful of sand. He laughs at me. And then he's on me, fast as a panther. He is choking me. I claw at his arms, draw blood. He doesn't seem to notice. He tightens his grip on my throat, and I can't breathe. My heart is racing. I gulp for air. I know that I am going to die right then, in this stranger's stranglehold, alone in this barren desert.

A little girl appears on an amusement park ride. She watches me struggle and says nothing. I look closer and I see that she has my mother's face and then she has my sister's face and then she has Heather's face.

"Help me," I croak in what I believe is my final breath.

She fades out, disappears. My throat is burning. The man I have been fighting is gone. I lie alone in the sand, my chest heaving. I feel dirty and empty and defeated. Mostly, though, I feel alone.

When I walked out of the hospital Monday morning, I learned that my court case was going to be held in Santa Barbara. An hour later, I was aboard a bus chugging up the coast to Santa Barbara County Jail, where I would be confined until I got my final sentence. I knew that this stretch was no quick hitter. I had served eighteen months of my three years the last time. I expected double that haul, maybe less if I had a good lawyer. Unfortunately, I couldn't afford a good lawyer. The state assigned me a real dump truck, a rumpled old guy who looked like he'd gotten his law degree before we had laws. I had to count on getting lucky. And Camp Snoopy again was no automatic. They might want to send me to a tougher spot, to deliver a message.

Before they loaded us onto the bus, the cops offered us snacks and sodas for the ride. I asked if I could see the *Herald-Examiner.* As the bus merged onto the Ventura Freeway, I stretched out in the back, fingered the paper, scanned the headlines, and pulled out the sports section. I read Malamud's column and then I turned to what I really wanted to know: the results of Sunday's pro football games. I felt around in my pocket and took out the crumpled newspaper I'd ripped out from Thursday. I flattened out the page and looked at the games I had circled. A couple of the games had been smudged by my sweat. Didn't matter. I could still make out every game I'd circled. Using my middle finger as a guide, I checked each winning team with each of my circled teams. And I counted out loud:

"One and oh. Two and oh. Three and oh. Four and oh . . ."

Until I reached the last game and saw that I had gone 10-0. Didn't need the six points in any of the games, either. Ten and zero. I'd won them all. Every fucking one. I would've come home from Vegas with a hundred grand, debt free, every check covered, a free man.

I shook my head and went over the winners one more time. Yep. No mistake. Ten and oh. I'd won them *all.*

And that's when I realized that not only did God exist, He had a sly sense of humor. I looked up at the ceiling of that battered bus and I said aloud, "Very funny. Got me good this time. Got me *good.*"

I threw back my head and burst out laughing, and I didn't stop until we reached the jail. I laughed like I had never laughed before, big, dangerous laughter, the kind that pierces your side and steals your breath. And then half the inmates on the Goose started laughing with me. For no reason. No reason at all.

Look up Santa Barbara, California, in any guidebook, and you'll see photographs of a quaint coastal town, historic Spanish missions, and spectacular sandy beaches populated by breathtaking surfer babes in string bikinis. What you won't see are pictures of Santa Barbara County Jail, home of some of the meanest motherfuckers who have ever walked the earth.

The county must've felt that these guys needed religion because priests and ministers streamed in on an hourly basis. I wanted a turn, too, so I asked for a rabbi. Two weeks later a rabbi from a local Hillel showed up. He was a young guy just out of rabbinical school. Turned out he had been at Hillel at the University of Texas and he knew my brother Neal. We clicked after that. I asked him to bring me a *Chumash,* a Jewish bible, and a *siddur,* a prayer book.

I was beginning a search and I was desperate for answers. That moment—the moment I'd gotten arrested—was nothing less than *profound*. I'd had an awakening. I don't know how else to put it. It was divine inspiration. A moment of prophecy. I felt I was being led back, back to the tradition, back to Torah. I can't even say how I knew that. I just knew.

And most of all I knew that I had to abandon the life I was living. I could no longer live in fear. I couldn't live in anger. I couldn't be a criminal. I couldn't fuck people over anymore. I was done. So *done*.

I stayed at Santa Barbara County for two months. I have no idea what my attorney was doing, why he couldn't get me out of there and into Chino. I had the sickening feeling that he was arguing to get me more time instead of less. The judge wouldn't let me fire him, and he wouldn't let me argue my own case. I finally told my attorney to take the best deal and get me the hell out. I was going crazy in that jail.

The judge offered three years and eight months. I grabbed it. The guards pulled me out of the Santa Barbara cage and shipped me by Gray Goose to Chino, where I was to await final assignment.

They put me in a hole in Chino, a two-man, and told me that I was probably going to be shuttled to another facility.

I was heartsick. I wanted to stay. It didn't help that at meals and in the exercise yard, I could hear the inmates laughing at me. "Yeah, that's Borovitz. Said he'd never come back. Let's see where he ends up now."

One blistering day on the yard, I sat alone at a picnic table reading the *Herald.* I was focused on the sports section, reading a breakdown of all the baseball teams as they headed into spring training. This was always a great time, the time when every baseball fan is filled with hope. I was no different. This was going to be the Indians' year.

"Hello, Mark."

I immediately recognized the gentle voice of Rabbi Silverman. I looked up from the paper. The sun hit my eyes and caused me to squint. I made a visor out of my hand and shielded my eyes. Mel's face was in shadow. He looked like a spirit. He stood over me.

"Still checking the sports pages, huh? The betting lines?"

"I always got an interest," I said.

"I guess nothing's changed." Mel spoke softly, heavily.

I tossed the paper aside.

"Everything's changed, Rabbi," I said. "This time everything's changed."

I told him the story of my arrest and how I'd felt divine intervention. He listened, nodded, swayed slightly. It looked as if he were praying. When I finished, neither of us spoke. I said, "You don't believe me, do you?"

Mel shrugged. Not a statement, a reflex.

"I know," I said, "it sounds crazy."

"I've been around a long time, Mark. You hear a lot of things, lot of stories—"

I swallowed. "So I guess that's it. I guess you're gonna cut me off like everybody else."

Mel's face appeared out of the shadows.

"You got it all wrong, Mark," he said. "I'm not going to cut you off. You're a Jew. You're one of us. I won't let you go. That is my promise to you. I will never let you go."

I tried to speak and I couldn't. I wanted to tell Mel that the only person in my life who had made that same promise to me was my father.

My lip started to quiver and I began to cry. In the middle of the prison yard, on that oven of an afternoon, I sat hunched over at the picnic table and I sobbed. The tears tore down my cheeks like shards of glass.

I stood up and threw my arms around Rabbi Mel Silverman and I held on to him. I crushed him with my weight, the weight of my body and the weight of my soul. I couldn't help it. Because I couldn't let go.

"I'm sorry, Mel," I said. "I'm so sorry."

"It's all right, Mark."

As I clung to him, the tears and sweat streaming down my face, I lost track of time.

Still, Mel Silverman did not let go.

"It's all right, Mark," he said again. "It's going to be all right."

I was sent to Avenal, a new facility near Bakersfield, California, one of the hottest places on the planet, a buzzard's throw from Death Valley. Avenal was so new they hadn't even sorted the inmates into assignments. Everyone got the same job: busting up the ground to prepare it for planting grass.

So there I was, baking in Bakersfield, blasting away at dirt that was harder than cement. Now, I never complain about hard work. I love to work. I typically put in an eighteen-hour day; a twenty-hour day is not uncommon. I'm telling you . . . I *love* to work. And I am driven. Gotta make up for lost time.

However . . . busting up that earth in Avenal? That was just stupid. And at that time I tipped the scales at well over three hundred pounds. I was a man mountain. There I was in the scorching sun, slapping my silly shovel at the rock-hard earth. It was a fucking joke. So I did what I had to do.

I faked a heart attack.

I threw myself on the ground, grabbed my left arm, and starting panting like a dog. Within minutes, I was hustled into the prison ambulance and we were speeding over to the hospital ward. I recovered quickly. I didn't want some prison surgeon with an itchy scalpel finger getting any bright ideas. Then I caught a break. The medical technician assistant (MTA) who attended me remembered me from Chino. She was a big woman herself with a pink punk hairdo. She studied my chart on her clipboard and clicked her tongue.

"What's the matter, you don't like beating up the ground with a toy shovel in a million-degree heat?"

I grinned. "It's one of my favorite things to do. Right up there with running marathons."

"We're just trying to beautify our new state facility," she said. "Gonna be gorgeous when they put the grass down."

"I hope I live to see it."

She flicked her finger against my chart. "How you feeling now, Mark?"

"Better. Don't know how long I'm gonna last without my meds, though."

"Yeah, I see on your chart you had a prescription. Problem is, we don't have our own pharmacy yet."

"I bet that's gonna be beautiful, too."

"I bet," she said.

She leaned over and pressed her palm against my fore-head. "No fever, Big Guy."

"I'm getting hot, though."

"You are a charmer."

She kept her hand there for a few more seconds, then took it away and scribbled something on my chart. "I just signed for your meds," she said. "Doc has to approve it."

"That a problem?"

She shrugged. "Not for me."

She winked. My laugh followed her out the door.

NEAL

When our father died, I not only lost him, I also lost my brother. It happened slowly. I wasn't totally aware of it at the time. There are three and a half years between us. And the year my father died, I went away to college. Then I went to Israel, and after I graduated college, I went back to Israel. So there were literally years in which Mark and I didn't have any meaningful time together. We weren't even in the same country.

I never knew the details of Mark's life. I knew there was trouble. My mother and my uncle Harry were very protective of Mark. Uncle Harry would always help. He would cover Mark's bad checks. Then Mark started getting in more trouble and he moved to California and became even more estranged from him. I would try to talk to him, try to get him straight. He wouldn't listen. He would turn me off. We were living at opposite spectrums. I was in rabbinical school and he was living a life of crime.

I didn't know what to make of Mark. I was embarrassed by him. The truth is, when people asked me about my family, I'd tell them that I had one brother and one sister. I wouldn't mention that I had another brother. If I ever met someone from California who told me he'd met my brother Mark, I'd just say, "How much?"

When Mark first went to Chino, I wrote to him. The letters he wrote back were superficial. We really didn't connect. The second time, though . . . it was different. He had changed. Truly. He started asking me for books. So I sent him some. He read those and he wanted more. He couldn't get enough. That was how we began to reconnect. Through books. That became my T'Shuvah: reconnecting with my brother. That's how I did it. I became his book dealer.

And then, once again, I became his brother.

I couldn't wait for my brother's books. I read them as soon as they arrived. I devoured them. I felt like a starving man who's suddenly discovered a buffet.

I read all day and into the night. Guys screamed at me to shut out my light. Sometimes I ignored them and sometimes I honestly didn't hear them. I was struck by the newness of what I was reading. I was like a little kid who was learning to read for the first time. I was moved and enlightened and amazed. I lingered over certain passages, reading them over and over, always finding something deeper, something I'd missed.

I learned that the Torah wasn't an abstract work at all. It was a living text, the ultimate guide to life. It was a path to everything. It told you how to sleep, how to eat, how to walk . . . all leading up to how to *be.* I learned that physical action was more profound than mental or even spiritual action. Your actions could actually lead to spiritual growth. You can impact the world, you can even *correct* the world by new action, by redemption, by *T'Shuvah*. When I read these things, I felt them. And I started to see. It was as if I had been living with a kind of film over my eyes and now the film was starting to dissolve.

About a month into my reading, I was shuttled over to Los Angeles County for my court case. This was it. I would appear in front of a judge who would decide what to do with my current sentence. As I stepped into the courtroom and made my way toward the bench, I noticed the judge's nameplate. I couldn't believe my eyes. I'd gotten a Jewish judge.

I whispered to my lawyer, "Don't turn this into a three-ring circus. Let's try to keep my sentence at three years, eight months, and hit the road."

"I'll handle it," the lawyer said.

First thing, he started into a song and dance. I could see the prosecutor standing on the other side rolling his eyes. My lawyer had definitely seen too many lawyer shows on TV. He finished his argument with some dumb emotional plea that turned his face bloodred.

The judge turned to me. "You have anything to add, Mr. Borovitz?"

I *was* catching a break. The Jewish judge was giving me the chance to plead my own case.

"Your Honor, I would just like to say that I know I've made a mistake . . . *many* mistakes. Those are in the past. I'm changing. I really, truly am. I've begun to study and read the Torah and other Jewish teachings. I know that this reading and these works are having a deep effect on my life. I can tell you that I am undergoing a drastic and profound rehabilitation.

I know it will take time. And I am going to put in that time. I regret everything that I've done and I promise you I am in the process of starting a new life."

The judge paused for a second, took in what I said, then nodded at the prosecutor.

"Your Honor," the prosecutor said, "Mr. Borovitz is a professional con man. He's had an FBI file since 1967. He's got an arrest record that's longer than *War and Peace*. When he was released from prison just over a year ago, he managed to break his parole almost immediately. I was unmoved by his statement to you because I know that he's just trying to work his con, even to you. I see no indication of change, rehabilitation, a new life, none of that. Don't see it, Your Honor."

The judge nodded again. He had an angular face and a rabbinical beard. He wore thick glasses, which he now took off. He pinched the bridge of his nose, blew on the lenses of his glasses, wiped them on the sleeve of his robe, put them back on, and peered over the frames at me, as if he were peeking over a fence.

"Mr. Borovitz," he said, "I'm sentencing you to an additional eight months."

"You're giving me four years, four months? Your Honor—"

"Case dismissed," he said. He slammed down his gavel.

"This is for *checks*, Your Honor."

"Let's go, Mark," my lawyer said circling his hand around my biceps.

"It's not right," I hissed at my attorney. "It doesn't make any sense."

"It's out of your hands."

My lawyer steered me out of the court, into a hallway. A guard came up behind me and snapped a pair of handcuffs over my wrists. He led me out to the street where a van idled, waiting to take me back to Avenal.

I felt railroaded. Abused by the system. What chance did I have? I had a court-assigned, washed-up attorney going up against a slick, Ivy League–educated prosecutor and a Jewish judge who must have thought I was bad for the religion and needed to be taught a lesson. Talk about a no-win situation.

And then I realized that my lawyer was right. There was nothing I could do. It was out of my hands. I had to play the hand I was dealt and play it the best way I could.

I dove back into my reading. I started taking notes, keeping a journal. I started relating to the narrative of the Torah, especially the story of Passover. I discovered profound parallels between the Passover story and the story of my life. I began to personalize the text. The Torah became about me. It was all there: slavery, bondage, survival, redemption, and, finally, freedom. I even equated the building of Pharaoh's pyramids with the breaking of the ground outside Avenal so the prison could have new grass.

About a week later, my friend, the punk MTA, came for a visit. She was smiling.

"I have a proposition for you," she said.

"Does it involve you, me, and a bottle of champagne?"

"Sorry. It only involves a transfer to Chino."

"Really?"

"It's unbelievably expensive to ship your meds up here with no pharmacy on-site. We're sending a busload of people over to Chino. If you want to be on that bus—"

"You kidding? What do I have to do?"

She smiled. "Ask nice."

"Please," I said. "Pretty please."

"I'll miss you, Big Guy," she said.

"Me, too. Any chance you can rush it?"

"Hey, we're flirting here."

"I'm a married man, you know that."

"Sigh," said the MTA. "All the good ones are taken."

I later learned that Mel Silverman had a lot to do with transferring me out of Avenal. He also had a lot to do with getting me into a two-person cell. This was a luxury usually reserved for only the best and worst prisoners. My cellmate was a guy named Joseph. He was a young Jewish guy in his twenties, very odd, smart, shy, and aloof. Joseph also liked to read. What was creepy was that he liked to watch me read. I don't mean watch for a couple of minutes, either. I mean for *hours*. I'd tell him to cut it out or I'd body slam him into the wall. That didn't scare him. He'd just keep staring. Finally, I gave up trying to get him to stop and I just let him look.

As it turned out, I wasn't in the cell much, anyway. Mel managed to get me a job as an assignment clerk, and then a few weeks later when the rabbi's clerk left, Mel switched me and I became his full-time clerk.

As prison gigs go, this was a dream. I typed letters, ordered books, kept schedules; I did whatever Mel needed. I also began going to services Friday nights and Saturday mornings. One Friday, Mel couldn't be there, so I led services myself. After that, whenever Mel had another commitment on *Shabbos,* I'd take over. I'd round up as many Jews as I could. I'd ask them to come to services as a favor to me and to Mel. When that didn't work, I'd bribe them with bagels.

One afternoon, I was sitting in Mel's office, struggling with a passage in the Torah, and Mel walked in.

"What do you have there?" he asked me.

I showed him. I scratched the top of my head. "Rabbi, we gotta start studying. I need help with this."

He seemed a little hesitant, a little dubious. "What do you want to study?"

"I don't care," I said. "Anything."

"Well, what do you want to learn?"

"I want to learn how to be *better*."

"All right," Mel said. "We'll study."

MEL

"*He meant it. He was intent on ceasing his former criminality. He wasn't sure how to do it. Wasn't sure which way to go. So we began studying together. A couple times a week. Sometimes more.*"

Mel leans forward, rests his elbows on his knees. He speaks quietly, as if he is about to reveal a secret.

"*At first I wondered, you know, what was his real interest? Did he have an angle? Was this a con of some sort? I thought that. I mean, he had a history, and this was a pretty remarkable shift. Quite a turnaround. Well, he became an avid student. He took initiative with the group, selected passages, helped me. 'Rabbi, I think the guys would like to hear this. They need to hear this.'*"

Another shake of the head. "*I'd been with the institution for fifteen years at the time. You think you know what the inmates will give you—*"

Mel Silverman waits, remembers.

"You don't always know," he says in wonder. "You don't always know."

Mel clears his throat and nods. "In a way, Mark became an assistant rabbi. He put together a kind of Jewish chapter at Chino. He ran things. He organized services, got things going around the Holidays. And he got more and more into Torah. He wanted to advance. He has a fine mind, a very discriminating mind. He was using it to get into greater depth with the text, with the teachings. It was a glorious thing to watch, and to be part of."

Mel cranes his neck toward the ceiling. His eyes glisten as he sorts out what he is about to say.

"There were two breakthroughs. Two major events. The first one occurred one time when we were having a discussion. We were talking about seeing God and I said, 'Moses was the only one to see God face-to-face.'

"A couple days later, Mark came back and said, 'Rabbi, I think you're mistaken. I think Jacob also saw God face-to-face.'

"I said, 'Show me the text.'

"'Right here. Where Jacob wrestles with the angel.'

"I looked where he was pointing. Mark truly identified with Jacob. Saw himself as someone who wrestled with angels and demons, someone who got down into the dirt. Jacob was him and he was Jacob. It's very powerful when you identify with a main character in a book and Mark had found his alter ego in the Torah. Jacob.

"I said, 'Well, Mark, you're pretty close. This indicates God's face. It's an aspect of God, not exactly like Moses, who clearly, the text states, saw God face-to-face. You found something here, though. I stand corrected, Mark.'

"Oh, did he feel good. Confident. He had one-upped the

rabbi. He left our discussion that day beaming, absolutely beaming. He couldn't wait to come back and challenge me again. I was so proud of him. I was beaming right back. This was a defining moment for him. A turning point. Mark's faith stemmed from Jacob. If Jacob the heel could see God's face, maybe there's hope for me."

And now Mel pauses. "I suppose it was a miracle, all of it. In twenty-five years as an institutional chaplain, a prison rabbi, I've had exactly one true success story: Mark's. Truthfully, it had little to do with me. I happened to be there. I was merely a conduit. An ear. A resource. I was open and willing, I'll admit that." He grins shyly. "I helped."

And the other event, the other breakthrough?

"This was when I knew that Mark was really serious about his studying, about his transformation. One afternoon, after we'd been studying for some time, I said to him, 'Mark, I want to get rid of the refrigerator. What do you think?'

"It was like asking him to give up his left arm. At least that's what I thought. That's what it would have been like before, during his first time at Chino.

"'Fine, let's get rid of it,' he said. 'We don't need it. It's a distraction.'

"When he said that, I knew it was real. I knew he was really changing."

I knew that I couldn't climb out of the pit alone. I needed somebody who would help me up, who would wrestle with me, who would wrestle with my soul. Someone who would force me to face the lies I was telling myself.

Rabbi Abraham Joshua Heschel said that one of the great passions of human beings is our ability to deceive ourselves.

I was a master at deceiving myself. I had a gift for it. I could deny the obvious even when it was shoved right in my face.

Mel Silverman was the one who made me wrestle my own soul and he made me wrestle with him. He made me confront all the shit in my life, and he made me see that my life wasn't all shit. He was a master wrestler himself because he was tenacious and he was kind, and once he saw that this time I wasn't going to give up, he never let me go.

I know there were guys in prison, inmates, who were suspicious of me. I can understand their doubts. There are a lot of con men in prison. Lot of guys trying to figure ways to get plum assignments. They saw being a religious newborn as a way out. I heard rumblings that I wasn't for real. They called it hiding behind God's cloak. "Borovitz is using this religion thing. It's just another one of his hustles."

I couldn't do anything about what they were thinking. I found myself more and more alone. I did my job, hung out with the Jewish guys, tried to keep my focus. I got very charged, very energized. I wanted to learn. That became my action and my fight. I fought to replace my self-deception with self-discovery. That's what it was all about for me. Hearing the music of my soul. Hearing the music.

I could hear God speaking to me. I'm serious. Dead serious. In the Torah, God speaks. How do we know? We just know. So there I was in prison doing my time for crimes I had committed, and I knew that this was not a moral problem. It was a spiritual problem. I knew that this was deep in my soul, not in my psyche, in my soul.

I began to work on my soul. I started the search for my essence. I had to learn to listen to my soul instead of listening to my mind and to the bullshit I could sell myself. I knew this was no overnight thing. I knew that I wasn't going to just hear some truth and it would be "Abracadbra! Wow! I'm changed! I'm a new man!" I knew that nobody was going to slap me on the forehead and yell "Heal!" and that would be that. It doesn't work like that. It is a life process. It began for me in prison and it continues to this day and will continue all my days, a constant and messy and difficult wrestling. And I have to keep a constant awareness. I have to always be on high alert. We all do. Both internally, our unconscious or subconscious, and externally, our deeds.

I wrote down all of Mel's teachings in a notebook. And I tried to change how I lived my life. Slowly, I saw changes in myself. *Slowly.* It took me a while to lose my hustle. I still ached for action. I was still betting on football, booking bets. And I was still hustling food. There was a different emphasis, though. I was experiencing a shift. I used food to get the Jewish cons to come to Mel's classes or Friday night services. Sometimes you need a draw to get people to move in your direction. Regular meals at Chino were inedible slop, a disgrace. I knew that if I could offer decent eats, the Jewish guys would come and they might stay for services. It usually worked.

I still operated on the edge sometimes. Mel was the rock behind me, though. Even when he wasn't there physically, I could feel his presence pulling me away from the edge, back to solid ground. I didn't want to let him down. I developed this intense loyalty and love for him. I became his representative in the yard. I vowed to live up to his name.

Prison life was a never-ending, constantly moving con game. You hustled for food, for smokes, for every favor and privilege you could imagine. I knew I would have to let all that go eventually. For now, I was content to differentiate between conning to survive inside and scamming people and writing bad checks on the outside. I knew I was done with that shit forever.

Still, I had my hustle when I needed it.

There was this guy in the Aryan Brotherhood named Whitey. Whitey was buff, a wall of muscle. All he did was lift weights and hassle Jews. That was his day. He was a prick. A real piece of shit. He'd extort money from the Jewish guys. He even got them to give him stuff from their monthly canteen—food, razors, cigarettes, anything he wanted. Then he started coming around the chapel and acting like a total asshole. He had the idea that Jews were weak and wouldn't put up a fight. Whitey was wrong.

The R&R clerk happened to be a Jewish guy, a friend of mine. R&R stood for receiving and release. In English, transfers. One night I told my friend about Whitey. We decided to send Whitey on a little trip. We typed up a transfer form and purposely left off the destination. Then we typed another one. And another one. We covered Whitey's Aryan ass with a fucking *mound* of paperwork. Drowned him in it. Then we sent off the forms.

The next morning, two guards rousted Whitey out of his bunk and stuck him on a bus. The bus drove him to another joint in the state. Problem. When Whitey tried to enter that prison, the administration had no destination paper on him and they wouldn't let him in. Figured he got sent to the wrong joint. They shoved him back on the bus and sent him to another joint. The bus got there, same result. Poor Whitey. He traveled on that same bus for one solid month. He visited every prison in the state before the brilliant powers that be figured out that someone was fucking him over and he was never supposed to leave Chino. By the time he got back, he hadn't slept in a bed or eaten anything except soggy energy bars for something like six weeks.

Soon as he returned to Camp Snoopy, he sent one of his guys to the chapel to see me. I came out when I was good and ready. Whitey was standing in the yard. He had bags under his eyes the size of Samsonite luggage.

"You don't look so good," I said.

"Listen, man," he said. His hands were trembling and his voice was cracking. "I was an asshole. I'm sorry. I won't fuck with none of the Jews ever again, I promise. I won't do nothing. Me and you? We're cool. Just please don't ever put me on another bus."

"I don't know what you're talking about."

"Please. I'm asking you."

"Whatever. I'm just glad we don't have any problems, me and you."

I watched him stagger away, his knees buckling whenever he took a step. I coughed to keep from laughing out loud.

Mel and I really got into it. We studied Torah and Talmud. We read Maimonides and the works of Rabbi Akiva and other Jewish scholars and thinkers. We argued and wrestled over words and passages and interpretations. I felt high. Higher than when I was drinking. This was verbal combat and I got off on it. Mel was a master. He was intellectual and he was tough. He knew how to deal with my con artist bullshit. He wouldn't give in to me. I was a wild man. It's always been tough for me to sit still. I'd pace like a caged animal, walk around the room, holler, bang the table with my fist.

"This doesn't make sense!" I'd shout. Mel would just smile and point out another way to look at it, show me another door to walk through. One thing I loved about studying Torah. The more questions you ask, the more questions you'll find.

I would always come back to Jacob. I identified with him so deeply. Jacob was a con man and a thief and a hustler. And he changed. He struggled to find the balance in his life. Finally, he did. He became respected, a leader. I believed that if a reformed lowlife like Jacob could turn out so well, there was hope for me.

One day I got a letter from Heather. She was seven years old. The envelope was addressed in her half-printing, half-cursive style. I broke into a huge smile when I saw it. I tore open the envelope and I read:

"Daddy, I hate you. I hate you because I love you and you're a part of me and I'm a part of you. When you're in jail, I'm in jail and I didn't do anything to go to jail for. I hate you for that. It's not fair. Love, Heather."

I read the letter again. And again. I kept on reading it, over and over, countless times. I read it again and I realized that I had it memorized. I folded it neatly and I put into my wallet. I needed to talk to her.

It wasn't easy to make a collect call. It cost money or cigarettes, and I had given up my regular hustle, so I didn't have much left to barter with. I called in some favors, made a bunch of deals. I promised to write a stack of appeal letters for a dozen illiterate cons. That got me enough cigarettes to call Heather.

At this time, around mid-1987, Linda and I were going through the worst of it. During my first stay in Chino, she and Heather came to visit me every weekend. This time, she didn't come very much. It was hard for me. Saturdays and Sundays, most people had visitors. I had no one. I'd see inmates with their families and I'd feel a hole inside me. Not seeing Heather was killing me. I had to talk to her . . .

I made the call. Linda accepted the charges. We spoke briefly. We didn't have much to say to each other. After a brutally awkward pause, she handed the phone to Heather.

I told her I had gotten her letter and that I was very sorry. And I told her that she was right, everything she said in the letter was right. I told her that even though she was much younger than I was, she was much smarter. I swore to her that I had changed. I was studying and reading and I was a different person. She would see. I told her that I loved her more than anything in the world and that I would never go away again. Ever. I swore that on my life.

She didn't believe me. How could she? So far, I'd shown her a consistent pattern of lies and bullshit. I couldn't just tell her that I'd changed and expect her to believe me. I had to show her.

When I hung up, I felt a new drive. I had to change for Heather. I had to change for my daughter, who both loved me and hated me and was right about both feelings. And whenever I would feel myself slip, I would open my wallet, pull out her letter, and read it aloud.

When you're in jail, I'm in jail.
Seven words.
Seven words that changed my life.

8

Return

MEL

Mel Silverman taps his fingertips against his lips.

"You know what they say about Rabbi Akiva? Forty years he was yom ha'aretz, an ignorant Jew. Unknowledgeable and unethical, that's what yom ha'aretz means. He hated the rabbis. Resented them. Then at forty he became a rabbi. The story goes that he lived to be a hundred and twenty. He started off as a tanner. The lowest-ranking job. It stinks. A stinking job. Pulled himself up from the very bottom. When Akiva became great, he came into Jerusalem in triumph, surrounded by his disciples. His wife, Rachel, was with him, off to the side. He stopped. The disciples wanted to move on. Akiva said, 'Hold it.'

"He looked over at Rachel, looked over at his wife, and according to scholars, said to the crowd around him, 'Whatever I am is because of her. Whatever you are is because of us. And whatever you have is because of knowledge, because of Torah.'

"I think Mark would say the same about Harriet."

HARRIET

*She sits at her desk in her wide spacious office. The decor is
earthy and calming, and the furniture is rich and comfortable.
She is trim in a rust-colored business suit. Her hair is a blur of
red and brown, cut close, slicing down across her forehead. Her
cheekbones are high and full, Hepburn-esque. Her smile is
electric.*

*In this space, command central, she is in control. She rocks
rhythmically in her chair, in a liturgical rhythm, unconsciously,
as if she is praying. She exudes pride and strength.*

And then she speaks.

*Her voice is deep, resonant, and sexy. Her throaty alto is in
perfect harmony to his clear baritone. And when Harriet talks,
you hear a kind of music. What's more, you listen.*

You must.

*E*ighty-four. That's when I first met him. I was a social
worker, visiting the prison. We were all in line, a group of
us, waiting to squeeze in. Mark's wife was there and the two
children. They had brought him kugel. A big aluminum foil
tin of kugel.

We didn't have much contact. He was huge. A bear. Tough
looking, with a shaved head and a scowl. Not somebody I
wanted to know. I saw him again a few years later. I had just
started Beit T'Shuvah downtown. That came about because I
was constantly visiting all these cons and they would all say
the same thing, "I want to change. Where can I go when I get
out? There is no place for me. Nowhere to go."

I would try to find something for them through Jewish
Family Services or other agencies. There was nothing. Not even

*beds for the night. It became so frustrating that at some point I
just said, "Fuck it. I'll just start my own place."*

*FEMA, the Federal Emergency Management Agency, was
offering grants so I wrote a proposal. The people who hired me
for my social worker job were part of Gateways Hospital. So I
wrote a proposal through them to house Jewish people coming
out of jails and prisons. I got a grant to buy a property. That's
all I got. I got no operating funds, no money for furniture, for
staff, nothing. I said, "Fine, I'll buy a house. I don't need staff.
I'll be the staff. I'll move in."*

So that's what I did.

Big mistake.

*I set up and I moved a couple of guys in. The first week
they stole all my jewelry, including my gold bracelet from my
confirmation. That's when I realized I couldn't do this by myself. I thought it would be so easy. I'd make chicken soup and
they'd all behave. Uh-uh.*

*Right after I opened my doors, I got a phone call from
Rabbi Silverman. He told me the men had concerns about
how I was running Beit T'Shuvah. They weren't sure it was
meeting their needs. They wanted to talk to me.*

*I went out to the chapel at Chino and sat down with them.
There were about fifteen inmates. Pretty loud guys. The loud-
est, by far, was Mark. He was their leader, their spokesman.
We were all sitting in a circle and he starts yelling, opening up
his mouth. I don't remember the particulars. Questions, challenges. "Are you doing this? What about that?"*

*Here was this big guy, this gargantuan inmate, attacking
me. And here are all these guys, his followers, lying around on
their asses, and I'm out there trying to help them and instead
of gratitude, they're giving me heat.*

Finally, after one of Mark's outbursts, I said to him, "Listen, I'm out there trying to make this work. If you know so much, smart-ass, when you get out of here, why don't you come help me?"

"Maybe I will," he says.

I didn't like this guy. Didn't like him at all. And I don't think he liked me.

About a month later, I'm sitting in my office and there's a knock on my door. I look up. It's him. This big guy standing there in a green running suit. I just stared at him. I was speechless.

"I'm here," he says. "I've come to help."

I was taken aback. I had put that challenge out there before and nobody ever took me up on it. Nobody ever came. He just showed up unannounced. Didn't call. Just showed up.

Got me.

My mother, Molly Katz, considered herself an intellectual. She read voraciously, loved poetry, enrolled in college at NYU. She quit when her father committed suicide. She was nineteen. A few years later she married my father, David Nadel, who was a lawyer. She was engaged to somebody else, a wealthy guy, and my father charmed her, wooed her, and she broke the engagement.

My father never practiced law. He couldn't find his place in life. He tried different things. He was a salesman, a shoe salesman actually. He did that for a while. He sold textiles. During the war he worked in a defense plant. He died very young. He was forty-four. I was fourteen. I was an only child and I suddenly felt alone, abandoned.

*My life has unbelievable parallels with Mark's. We were
the same age when our fathers died and for both of us, our fathers were the connection. The loss . . . it was incalculable.*

*Mark had his rebellion immediately. He became a gangster.
My rebellion was brewing inside me. I went to college. Tufts . . .
Jackson College for Women. My mother's choice. She wanted
me to marry a Harvard Law boy. She said, "Lawyers make
better husbands than doctors. Doctors keep bad hours and
they're unfaithful. In our family, we marry lawyers."*

*Sophomore year I found him. Gary Rosenzweig. He had
graduated Harvard Law and found a plum job. Clerking for
the chief justice of the Supreme Court of Minnesota. He was
a catch. He was a Democrat and he liked classical music.
Those were my conditions.*

*We had a traditional wedding. I ordered the china and the
silver, the whole thing. And at the age of nineteen, I moved
with my new husband to Minneapolis, to be a housewife.*

*The deal was, I had to finish college. My terms. I enrolled
at the University of Minnesota and majored in English. And
while my husband was off clerking for this Minnesota Supreme
Court justice, I was running wild at school. Running wild. My
rebellion had begun.*

*I was free. And I was in love with every one of my profes-
sors. I was a very naughty girl, living a double life. I acted
crazy all day, then I would come home and try to be this
housewife person with my china and my silver and those
damask tablecloths that were so far from anything that was
me. My husband and I would go out with other couples. Friday night we'd have dinner with his parents. Then I'd go
back to school and be this existentialist, intellectual girl who
was screwing all of her professors. It was fun.*

The marriage didn't last even two years. I was having

many, many affairs. And not just with my professors. Also with the husband of the couple we played bridge with. I was out of control. And I was in this world that I loved. Saul Bellow was there and John Berryman, the great American poet. To them, I was intriguing. I was this dark-haired New York intellectual bohemian. My competition was a bunch of Swedish farm girls.

I was finding a new part of me, a part that I enjoyed. I was in this club. The Smart Club, you know? It was very heady, very liberating, and very sexy.

I graduated from the University of Minnesota and nobody came to my graduation. My mother was angry with me. She hated what I'd done to my marriage, to my perfect Jewish Harvard Law School husband.

"You have made your bed, Harriet," she said. "Now you have to lie in it."

I stayed in Minneapolis and tried to figure out what to do with my life. Right after graduation, I got a phone call in the middle of the night from John Berryman. He had taken my phone number because he was going to call everybody who didn't have to take the final. Stalking the smart girls.

"Mrs. Rosenzweig?" he says. "John Berryman here. Can I come over?"

At three o'clock in the morning he arrived in my little one-room boardinghouse with a copy of Dream Songs, a bottle of gin, and a bottle of vermouth. This guy was three times my age. Big bear of a guy. He sat cross-legged on my bed, we passed the two bottles, and he read me his poems. Thus began my affair with one of America's greatest poets.

Meantime, I was out of money. I needed a job. What do you do with an English major and no husband? Anything you can. I found a job with the Girl Scouts of America. My job was called Field Director, which meant that I organized the cookie

sales and camping trips and helped with the volunteers. I actu-
ally found this brief period of my life rather funny. By day, I
was literally this Girl Scout, the green uniform and everything,
while at night, I was over at Berryman's apartment, getting
drunk, reading poetry, and doing the wild thing.

There was actually a pattern here. A desire for two lives,
and not a split so much as a desire for both. I couldn't choose. I
knew I should be with the good boy, the safe bet, the Harvard
Law guy, the nice kid who went to temple and worshipped his
parents. I was also deeply attracted to the bad boy, the tough
kid.

Mark, of course, was both. He was the good boy who be-
came a bad boy. Or was it the other way around? The gangster
rabbi. The nice Jewish boy criminal. Not too many of those. He
put it all together for me. I met my match with him. I mean
that literally. He was my match.

After a while, I left the Girl Scouts and somehow ended up
working for Jewish Family Services. I was always about saving
people. I was a missionary as a kid. I wanted to save the down-
trodden. I identified with the underdog. At first, I resisted this as
a career. Back then, you went to college and became a teacher.
That was the most common career path. With the guidance of
my boss, who became a kind of mentor, I decided to go to grad-
uate school and get a master's in social work.

During graduate school, I drifted away from Berryman,
who was spending most of his nights passed out in my apart-
ment, and I entered into a horrible, abusive relationship with
an antiquarian bookseller. He was this crazy guy. I couldn't
get away from him. It was a true nightmare. Hellish. Finally,
I called my mother, and she and my grandmother got on a
train and rescued me.

They offered me a trip to Europe and I took it. I went abroad for the summer. And somewhere between my first and second years of graduate school, I met Michael Rosetto, who lived in New York. He was very dark, very handsome. Exotic. Italian. This was my Italian period. I was taken in. His first name was Michaelangelo. He lived in New York and I'd always wanted to live there. So I came back from Europe, moved to New York, did the romantic New York thing, then married Rosetto and moved to the Upper West Side.

I couldn't shake my desire to save people. I took a job at the Henry Street Settlement House downtown, then I left and went to work at Fountain House, which was a kind of halfway house for people coming out of state mental hospitals. I would take them shopping and try to teach them how to live on their own. It was my first introduction to this sort of thing. The experience stuck with me. The difficulty and the reward. This is probably where the seeds for Beit T'Shuvah were sown.

Then I got pregnant, had a child, quit my job, and began a new life as a young married on the Upper West Side of New York. I could've been the cover girl for New York *magazine: private-school mom, shopping at Zabar's and Fairway Market, making trips to the Central Park Zoo, married to a successful engineer working at Rockefeller University.*

The truth is, I was stagnating. And I was indescribably lonely. One day, the elevator man knocked on my door. He looked like Denzel Washington. He had a joint.

He said, "You'll forgive me for being so bold. I was just wondering if you'd like to share this with me."

I let him in. One thing led to another. That was that. I started another rebellion. This one was my Black Power period. I moved off the Italians to the African-Americans. It was au courant. Bobby Kennedy and Martin Luther King were murdered. It was the great Smoke-In in Central Park, Nina Simone, Billie Holiday, all of it. Then it got ugly. The husband moved out, the elevator man moved in.

Meanwhile, I'm the PTA poster mom. Making birthday parties, reading in the classroom, dragging the kid to soccer games, all that shit. Double life. Split personality. My public persona, I'm as good as it gets. My home life, I'm living with a hood from Bedford-Stuyvesant.

And then it got totally insane and horrifying and dangerous. There were guns and cocaine and verbal abuse and physical abuse. I tried to move away with my daughter. That's when Elevator Man got really scary.

One afternoon, he brought three of his crew with him across the George Washington Bridge to my stepfather's law office, where my mother worked as a legal assistant. He walked in and pulled out his gun. He showed them a picture of my kid.

He said, "I want $5,000 or I'm going to hurt your grandchild."

They paid Mr. Elevator Man. They were also clever enough to mark the bills. The FBI was called. This was extortion across interstate lines. Federal business. Big stuff. I immediately had to get out of my house. I ran up Seventy-second Street, dragging my daughter, Elevator Man chasing me with a broken beer bottle. It was a horrible scene.

I left the country. My poor mother had to go to court and testify. It made all the papers. I finally escaped to California with my daughter. I followed my best girlfriend out here. Go West, young woman. I was starting a new life in the Land of Opportunity.

I took a series of social worker jobs. Nothing was really

fulfilling. I couldn't find my mission. The money was barely enough to scrape by on. I don't know . . . I was looking for something. Looking for a change. Looking for myself.

Then the Big Story.

I met this guy. He told me he was going to make me a millionaire. He was a real estate maven. His specialty was foreclosures. He started giving seminars. I left social work and followed him down to Orange County. I was his right hand, helping him with these seminars. I was beginning a whole new way of life.*

We started making a lot of money. A fortune. He worked this scheme: He'd let properties go and take all the equity out of them. I lived with him in his condo. I was the organizer and the motivator. I collected all the cash and he kept it. Once we hit the big number, the lottery as far as I was concerned, he said, get lost. Kicked me out.

I was stranded. My daughter had gone off to college and I was alone in Orange County. I had hit bottom. I had no money, no savings. I was forty-five years old and I was completely broke. I didn't know where to turn. Had no idea. I knew I had to do something, knew I had to change . . .

When I was running these seminars, I had started reading a lot of self-help and success literature. Science of the Mind, that sort of thing. A lot of people were going to a woman named Janet Levy. Her deal was "Expect a Miracle." Make your dreams come true. I always came at life from a different angle: Expect Nothing. Life is hard, then you die, the whole dark existential thing. That was how I saw it. Maybe it was the New York–L.A. thing. The scowl versus the happy face. I don't know.

I did know that I was penniless in San Pedro and all these peo-
ple around me were thinking positively and apparently living
good lives. I thought, "Maybe they're not so stupid after all."

I made an appointment to see Janet Levy. I was drawn to
her somehow. I was so confused and so desperate. I sat down
with her. She was a gentle soul, very soothing. It was a typical
L.A. la-la scene. Candles, incense. She looked at me. She had
great eyes. Caring, intelligent.

"Okay, Harriet," she said. "What do you want?"

"That's the whole problem," I said. "I don't know what I
want. If I knew what I wanted, I'd visualize it like every-
body else. I can't do that. I can't get there. The minute I try to
visualize, I'm done. I don't know what I want."

"Do you pray?"

That threw me. I squirmed in my chair. I sighed and I al-
most blew out one of the candles.

"Come on," I said. "Pray? I don't pray. I'm an intellec-
tual—"

"I'm going to pray for you," she said. Janet Levy closed her
eyes and put both of her hands over mine. "Father of the Uni-
verse, take this woman by the hand and guide her to her right-
ful voice. She knows she wants to do something meaningful.
She just doesn't know what it is yet. Please. Help her find her
place."

"Okay," I said, "that was interesting. Thank you."

I pulled my hands away and I left.

That was a Thursday afternoon. I was unemployed, un-
motivated, and stuck. Stuck in the mud. I couldn't get any
traction going.

The next morning I bought the paper and went right to the
classifieds. For some reason I wanted to see if there were any
social worker jobs advertised. And there it was. This little ad.

"Help wanted. Social worker with a Jewish background and culture to work with Jewish criminal offenders."

It was my moment. I knew it. Right there. My hands started to tremble. The hair on my arms stood up.

I said, aloud, "Shit. It worked."

The job, of course, was at Jewish Family Services. I applied, got it, never any doubt.

I believe that going to see Janet Levy and picking up that newspaper the next morning was divine guidance. My whole belief system was instantly shattered and reconstructed into something new, something positive, something stronger than my old belief system, which was made up of the negative voice, the voice that always said, "Who you trying to kid? That's not gonna happen. Never gonna happen."

That new belief has made all the difference in my life. I don't know if I believe that miracles happen, I don't know if I've come that far.

And then again, maybe I do believe in miracles. Hard not to believe when you look around here at Beit T'Shuvah.

That moment, though, for me, the timing of it . . . it is how I see the story of Mark and Harriet . . . how we both had these moments of spiritual clarity at the same time. If we hadn't, our paths would not have crossed.

We never would have met.

9

God Hustle

I left prison for the last time on my birthday, November 1, 1988. I was thirty-seven years old. I had served almost two years of my four years, four months sentence.

I moved into a halfway house near downtown L.A., a small clapboard California traditional on Grand Avenue in a neighborhood known for massive warehouses, vacant buildings, and gang warfare. The furniture in my one room was ripped and ratty and the carpet smelled of mold. Because of a technicality with my release, I wasn't allowed outside for the first two weeks. I was literally on house arrest. I spent those fourteen days talking on the phone to Heather, reading, studying, pacing, smoking, and staring out the window.

Mid-November arrived and the days grew gray and gloomy, a Cleveland sky over the L.A. skyline. The smog burned off at four-thirty and night fell at five. Through my window I'd watch the homeless people, junkies, dope dealers, drunks, and gangbangers congregating and posing at the street corner, and I would wonder who they once were and if I'd ever crossed paths with any of them in a bar, a car lot, or in prison.

On the last day of my two-week confinement, my parole officer came to see me with a list of what I could and could not do. He spoke low and as I strained to hear, my heart sank.

"How am I gonna find a job?" I said. "I have to tell every employer my prison record. I have to tell them I'm on parole. I can't work as a traveling salesman because I can't get a driver's license. I can't get a license to sell cars because I have a felony in the automobile business. I don't have a college degree. What am I supposed to do?"

"Guess you'll have to figure that out, won't you?"

He came back the next day and moved me from the halfway house to a reentry facility, another shabby halfway house near Vine and Franklin in the heart of Hollywood. There were mostly hookers, pimps, and starving actors on that street corner. Now, every morning, I would venture out and walk along Hollywood Boulevard, smoking and window shopping at pawnshops, tattoo parlors, and porno bookstores, trying to get a handle on my future.

During one of my walks I thought about the social worker who had visited us in Chino. She'd thrown down a challenge. Said if I knew so much, why didn't I see her when I got out and help her with her halfway house. Frankly, I didn't know what else to do. Harriet, her name was. Called me a smart-ass.

For some reason, thinking about her made me smile.

It took me a while to find Beit T'Shuvah. A forty-five-minute bus ride deposited me downtown and a short, meandering walk brought me to Lake Street. There it was. In the middle of the block. A large house looming in front of me, partially hidden by an immense, swaying palm tree. A rickety air-conditioning unit protruded from the left side like a giant nose. The main entrance was off to the right, up a few stairs, at the back of a wide porch. Heavy metal—Metallica or Guns N'

Roses—roared out of an open second-floor window. The house was a wreck. The roof was splotched, and shingles lay scattered over its peak like a bad toupee. The porch steps creaked as I climbed them. The screen in the front door was torn, and the paint on the walls was peeling away.

I walked in and the first sound I heard was Harriet's deep, melodic voice. I followed it down a hallway and found her in her office, talking on the phone. I waited until she finished her call, then I knocked on the open door. She turned to me and her mouth dropped open, like a puppet's.

I said, "I'm here to help."

She looked at me blankly.

"Remember? You said I should come see you when I get out. I'm out."

She started to say something, stopped, tried again. "Nobody's ever—"

And then I blurted out: "I need a job."

She hesitated. "Well, I could use someone to run the thrift shop. It's a mess."

"I'll take it."

"I can only pay you minimum wage. Five sixty an hour."

"I'll take it."

"I can't afford to pay you full-time. It'll have to be part-time for a while."

"I'll take it."

She smiled. "You said that, didn't you?"

I stepped all the way into her office. I looked out her window. Or tried to. It was entirely smudged in dirt. Looked as if it were smeared with chocolate.

"This place," I said, "is a dump."

"I know," Harriet said.

"I kind of like it."

As I rode the bus on my way to the thrift shop the next day, I took stock of my new life. I was living in one ratty room in the middle of freaked-out Hollywood; I had no car, license, checking account, savings account, or credit card, and almost no cash; I was on parole and about to start a job for minimum wage at a thrift shop. Thank God I was no longer at the *bottom*.

I thought about my daughter and my wife. On the weekends, I rode a different bus into the Valley to see Heather, who was now eight years old. I tried to tell her how much I'd changed. She didn't trust me. She put up an icy wall between us. I tried to break it down. It was hard going. I saw that it was going to take time, maybe years, to repair our relationship. I asked God for help, knowing that patience has never been one of my best qualities.

Then there was Linda. I didn't know what to do there. Didn't know what I wanted. I had evolved into this reborn Jew, trying to find my way through studying and reading Torah and Jewish ethics and Jewish history. Linda had no idea what I was talking about or who I was. She wasn't Jewish and had little interest in hearing about my conversion. She wanted to rewind time, to go back to when we first met. She wanted me back the way I was, the guy who used to flirt with her in the car dealership. She couldn't accept that I was no longer him. That guy was gone forever.

The truth is, we both knew that it was over between us. We just couldn't act on it. It was all too raw. She wasn't sure she could trust anything, even her feelings. She knew for certain that she couldn't trust me to do the right thing, no matter how many times I promised her that she could. She was frozen. Neither of us knew what to do, so we did nothing.

We left everything where it was, up in the air, and we waited; waited for time to take over and heal, waited to move closer together or farther apart, waited for a choice to be made for us. I think we both felt the same way. I can't really be sure. We never talked about it.

I opened the door to the thrift shop and let out a soft whistle. Harriet had been kind in her use of the word *mess*. It looked as if a hurricane had ripped through the place. Clothes, toys, toasters, blenders, books, dishes, and silverware were strewn together into a small teetering mountain. And that was just the first table. There were three more. I sighed and took a long swig of the coffee I held in my hand. Coffee had replaced booze as my drink of choice. Whenever I felt the urge for a drink, I'd grab a cup of coffee. I was up to ten cups a day, easy. I was wired. Like I needed more energy. I took another gulp of coffee, shivered from the jolt the caffeine gave me, and vowed right then to switch to decaf. I put the coffee down and rubbed my hands together like a safecracker. I dove into the pile on the first table.

It took me a week to organize the thrift shop. I sorted everything into categories, gave several bags of stuff away to the residents at Beit T'Shuvah, and tossed out bags of junk that were of no use to anybody. Then I determined a price for each item and made neat little price tags. I made everything affordable. I purposely priced a few things more than they were worth. I didn't really care if I got five bucks for the toaster that smoked when you put it on top brown. I just wanted to be able to *hondle*. I missed selling. I was entitled to a *little* fun.

After I spruced up the thrift shop, Harriet scheduled a

grand opening. She arrived one morning with all twenty of the Beit T'Shuvah residents. When she walked in, her face lit up.

"Where am I?" she said.

She browsed through the clothes table, then wandered over to the appliances. The smile never left her face. "I'm very impressed."

I bowed slightly. "Thank you."

She rubbed her hand over the side of the toaster. I'd polished it up. The thing glimmered. She leaned down and saw her reflection on the side.

"I can't resist a bargain," she said.

"Only five bucks. And that's not a bargain. That's a *steal*. It's worth double that, easy."

"Are you hustling me?"

I caught her grin in mine. "Me?"

"I'll give you two bucks for it."

"Two bucks? Forget about it. This baby gives you restaurant-quality toast."

"Two bucks. That's my offer." She stepped toward me. She'd cut the distance between us from two feet to less than a foot. I could smell her shampoo. Rain.

"Four-fifty," I said. I swallowed when I said it.

"Two-fifty. That's my final offer."

"Four bucks," I said. Somehow we were only a few inches a part now. "Buy it or lose it."

"Three dollars or I'm walking."

"You're a tough cookie," I said.

"You bet."

We were locked up in each other's eyes. I felt somewhere between dizzy and scared to death. Warm, too. Flushed. Borderline sweating.

"Sold," I said.

"Deal."

Harriet reached into her pocket, counted out three ones, and placed them in my hand. I closed my fingers gently around the bills and her fingers. She didn't move her hand for what seemed like forever. Finally, she pulled away and walked over to her toaster. She tucked it under her arm.

"That was fun," she said. "I have to admit, I thought you'd be a little tougher."

I shrugged. "I guess I'm out of practice."

"You didn't mind getting beat?"

"By you? Not at all."

And then she said quietly, "Maybe you can come over some time for a piece of toast."

"I'd like that."

She started to walk away.

"Oh, Harriet," I said. She stopped. "You need one more thing. I'll give it to you for thirty bucks. Can't use the toaster without it."

"Thirty bucks? For *what*?"

I gave her the widest smile in my arsenal. "A fire extinguisher."

Every morning before I went to work, Harriet and I would sit in her office, have a cup of coffee, and share our dreams. We'd talk about what Beit T'Shuvah could be, how we imagined it growing into a safe haven and spiritual community for recovering addicts, former convicts, anyone who was lost, abandoned, and without hope. We talked about our philosophies of recovery. I offered to lead a group. I wanted to talk to the residents about my experience as a con man and hustler and criminal. I wanted to share with them how my life led me to prison, how I'd hit bottom, how I discovered that the answers were within me, within my faith, how I was picked up off the basement floor by the hand of God, and how I struggled every day to maintain my balance. I wanted them to know that no matter what shit we've been through, no matter what kind of damage has been done to us, at some point we each have to take responsibility for ourselves. We can't rely on others and we can't blame others. We are alone, all of us, alone with God. I talked to Harriet about how I was now devoting my life to undo the damage I'd done to myself, to my family, to my soul. I asked her about *Shabbos* services at Beit T'Shuvah. She told me she'd hired a rabbi who came in twice a month.

"Why not do *Shabbos* every week?" I asked her.

"She can't come every week," she said.

"I'll do it." She tilted her head, considered this. "Why not? I can read the prayers, lead the services, do a little sermon, a little song, a little dance—"

Harriet laughed. "You're on."

I started leading services every Friday night. I admit, I've got a bit of showman in me. I made those services *rock*. I just let my passion out. I'd sing loudly and not always on key. I couldn't help it. Amazingly, the dozen or so residents who attended rocked out with me. Our services resembled a mini-revival meeting. Afterward, I arranged for a little *oneg*, a snack, some cake, and we'd do a *kiddish* with grape juice instead of wine. Pretty soon, Friday night services started creating a buzz. After a few weeks, all twenty of the residents started showing up. I decided to take the next step. I proposed to Harriet that I conduct a Torah study group. She agreed and I began holding a morning Torah session, Wednesday mornings at seven.

At the end of the day, I found myself wandering over to Harriet's office. I'd linger, making up any lame excuse to stick around. I'd empty her wastebasket, sweep the hall, lick stamps, anything. I noticed she didn't seem that eager for me to leave.

"Well," I said one night. I was out of stupid little things to do. "I'd better get over to the bus stop and catch the last bus home."

"Or we could grab some dinner and I could drive you home."

"Or we could do that," I said.

We stopped at Sizzler. I devoured a steak. She foraged through the salad bar. And we talked and talked, mostly about our lives. We discovered an eerie number of similarities. Incredibly, both of our fathers had died when we were fourteen. Their deaths had formed our lives, sending us both on long and winding soul searches. After a two-hour dinner that I never wanted to end, Harriet drove me back to the halfway house.

We sat in the car at my street corner. The windshield was fogged with our breath.

"This was really nice," Harriet said.

"Yeah. It really was."

I started to make a move toward her. I was awkward. Tentative. And I was nervous. Harriet turned away.

"You're married," she said.

"I know."

"So we're just going to be friends."

"Absolutely."

I felt like kissing her right then. I felt high, drunk, even though I hadn't had a drink in months.

"Friends," I said, and we shook hands as if we were

concluding a business deal. Except, unlike most business partners, we didn't let go.

"I was thinking," she said. "I live on First Street, right near Western and Beverly. It's not far from here. I can drive you in the morning. Save you forty-five minutes on the bus."

"That would be great. I could just come over. It's on the way. Then you wouldn't have to backtrack."

"Yeah. You could do that. I need a little extra time in the morning for beautification."

"You don't," I said, "need time for that."

She blushed. "So, okay, come over. I'll be your chauffeur."

"You sure?"

"Positive."

"Great. Thanks, pal."

I leaned over and kissed her on the cheek.

We began each day now in her apartment. I'd sit at her kitchen table, sip my coffee, and flip through the newspaper, while Harriet took a shower and got dressed. Every so often, she'd stop by the kitchen table for a sip of coffee. I'd read her the headlines and comment on the latest news. I'd bitch about how poorly my beloved Cleveland Indians were playing. We'd talk politics, books, movies, and show-biz gossip, and we'd discuss problems at Beit T'Shuvah. The conversation wouldn't stop at her kitchen table. We'd keep going on the drive in, and sometimes we'd grab a bagel and continue talking over breakfast in her office.

One evening over dinner, Harriet revealed the latest drama at Beit T'Shuvah.

"I need a secretary," she said.

"What happened?"

"Laurie fell off the wagon, hard. She got drunk and moved out. She's not coming back."

"What are you going to do?"

We were on dessert. It was late. Two waiters started stacking chairs. Another mopped the floor.

"I'm offering you the job," Harriet said.

"You want me to be your secretary?"

"Well?"

"I'm a little too heavy to sit on your lap."

"So I'll sit on yours."

"It's tempting," I said.

"It pays more. Eight dollars an hour."

"I'm talking about the sitting on the lap part."

"Is that a yes?"

"Yes, that's a yes."

We both grinned and once again we shook hands. This time I let go because my palms were sweating.

I became Harriet's right hand. I ran the office, collected the rents from the residents' families, and began working with Harriet on developing more outreach. I started calling temples and Jewish Community Centers. I would introduce myself over the phone. "My name is Mark Borovitz. I just got out of prison and I can help save kids in your community."

The phone calls clicked. The local Jewish community wanted to meet me. Harriet and I began setting up speaking engagements. She would talk about Beit T'Shuvah and introduce me, and I'd tell them my story. I'd pace and prance and shout and whisper and make the audiences laugh and scare the shit out of them. Afterward, a rabbi or synagogue president or Hebrew school principal would invariably tell me sad horror stories about one or more of their kids, usually from good families. They were stunned that this could happen in the Jewish community. Jewish kids are not supposed to be drug addicts or alcoholics or gamblers or thieves.

"I was a nice Jewish boy," I said. "I came from a good family. I went to Hebrew school and services every *Shabbos*. And look at me. It can happen to anyone."

I was touching a nerve. I'd get back to the office at Beit T'Shuvah after one of these speaking engagements and there would be a dozen phone messages asking me to speak somewhere else. It was heady and exciting and slightly unreal. I was still hustling; only now I was hustling for God.

While my work was heating up at Beit T'Shuvah, my personal life with Linda was approaching glacier status. We were not relating at all. I know that part of it had to do with what I was feeling for Harriet. And part of it had to do with what I wasn't feeling for Linda. I was confused and ridden with guilt.

One night I was home and I felt an urge I hadn't felt in months: I needed a drink. I walked down to Vine Street and went into a liquor store. I bought a bottle of VO, a bottle of vodka, and a package of Bloody Mary mix. I carried the stuff back to my apartment, tore open the bag, and mixed myself a strong Bloody Mary. I took one sip, let the thick pulpy mixture settle in my mouth, and swallowed. I nearly choked. I dumped the drink into the sink. I grabbed a water glass and poured in three fingers of VO. I took a sip. A sharp, bitter taste surged into my throat. It was like drinking paint thinner. I started to gag.

And then it hit me.

I was a drunk.

I knew that I drank a lot. I knew that I used to practically live in bars. I just never thought of myself as an alcoholic. Alcoholics were bums. They couldn't function the way I could. That's how arrogant I was. I couldn't hear my own message.

I stared at the bottle of vodka and the bottle of VO. I grabbed one in each hand and I dumped them down the drain at the same time. The next week I began going to AA meetings at Beit T'Shuvah. I had to. I needed help. I was an alcoholic.

I began losing myself in the study of Torah. I read the English translations, commentaries, related books, anything I could get my hands on. I struggled to find meaning in the vastness of the text, in the textures of the story. My study inspired and baffled me. Some of what I read spoke to my soul and some of it infuriated me. I wrote and called Mel Silverman. He did his best to teach me in his letters and over the phone. It was hard working with Mel this way, from a distance. The study of Torah doesn't work so well as a correspondence course. And the more I studied, the more questions, contradictions, and insights burned inside me. I wanted more.

At the suggestion of a friend, Harriet and I went to Hillel at UCLA one morning to hear a teacher named Jonathan Omerman. As soon as Jonathan spoke, I fell in love with him. He had a quiet, gentle manner. He was British and spoke with an intoxicating lilt. While his speech was soft, his thoughts were full of fire. He was dynamic, intelligent, and original. I was riveted.

I went over to Jonathan afterward and I introduced myself. I briefly told him my story. I saw his eyes fill up with sympathy and interest. I asked Jonathan if he would teach me, one-on-one. He agreed. We began meeting at his house. I would continue studying with Jonathan every week for the next five years.

Jonathan changed the way I looked at life. He made

religion *personal.* All of my studying started to click. I began to relate to God and Judaism in a way I had never envisioned. I saw my whole life—my past, my present, my losses, my loves, my failings, my successes, my sins, my good deeds, my rage, my empathy, all of it, all of *me*—as part of a whole. And I saw that all of these things, the good and the bad, were validated. As I worked with Jonathan, I felt an energy shift. An awakening.

One of Jonathan's lessons that resonated with me concerned the difference between essential pain and voluntary suffering. When you stub your toe, you experience pain, real pain, and that pain lasts however long it lasts. Depending on who you are, the *bitching* about the pain lasts a lot longer. The bitching about it is voluntary suffering. As long as we allow voluntary suffering to exist, we remain victims. We don't allow ourselves to experience the essential pain in proper measure, and then move on. I certainly knew all about voluntary suffering. I'd been suffering that way since the day my father died. It was time now for me to let go. Time to take the next step. I was no longer going to be a victim.

In late December, Linda called to invite me to a New Year's Eve party at her house. There was a different tone to her voice. She was warm and apologetic. She said that she'd been doing some thinking and that she wanted to start over. After all, we were a family, a bruised family, nevertheless, a family. She was having a few people over to celebrate the New Year. It was a new beginning and she wanted a new start.

I was torn. I wanted to spend New Year's Eve with Harriet. I wasn't sure where our relationship was headed; I just knew it was headed somewhere. The more time we spent together, the more I felt that we were soul mates. I was starting to envision a life at Beit T'Shuvah. I saw it as Harriet's baby, and my place. And sometimes, both when I was with her and when I was alone, I saw it as *our* place.

I admitted this to Harriet one night over dinner as I wavered between spending New Year's Eve with her or with Linda.

"There's no decision," she said. "You have to be with Linda. She's right. You have a family. It's important to be there for Heather. It sounds like Linda is trying."

I nodded, half-convinced. What I really wanted was to spend New Year's Eve with Heather and Harriet. That was a fantasy. I came back to reality and sucked it up, said good-bye to Harriet, and took the bus out to the Valley for New Year's.

Linda had gone all out. She'd decorated the apartment with streamers and balloons, made a cake, and bought several cases of good champagne.

That, of course, was problem number one.

As the party started up, I sipped decaf coffee while Linda's friends swigged bubbly out of plastic flutes. This was a first. I was the only sober person at the party. The whole evening was off, awkward. Most of Linda's friends weren't Jewish, and many were in the car business. They saw me as a tough guy. They romanticized my prison stay the same way we glamorize mobsters in the movies. Linda's friends wanted to find out about prison life. They wanted to hear my war stories. I was more interested in telling them how I'd found myself, how I'd hit bottom, and how I was working now to pull myself back up. I used the analogy of the Joseph story from the Bible when his brothers threw him into a pit and left him there. Joseph used all of his reserve and strength to climb his way out. My life was a pit, I told them, a cesspool of drinking and hustling and check-writing scams. God, I told them, reached down His hand and pulled me up. That's really the way I saw it. It was a miracle.

Linda's friends didn't want to hear any of this. They didn't want to hear about Joseph, or the Bible, or God reaching down His hand. They only wanted to hear funny and harrowing tales of prison life.

I wouldn't go there. I kept talking about how my life had changed, how my faith in God had gotten me through. I could see their eyes glaze over. They excused themselves. Left me standing alone with my decaf. I drifted from the kitchen into the living room into the dining room then back into the kitchen. I drank enough decaf that night to launch a ship.

I gave up trying to relate to Linda's friends and hung out with Heather in her room. We played a board game and I taught her how to play gin. She picked that up right away. First game she knocked with two and caught me holding fifty points. Second game she hit gin and stuck me with another fifty.

"You're a ringer," I told her. "A card shark. Just like me."

"Daddy, I'm winning a hundred to nothing. I'm way better than you."

I made a face at her. She started giggling and made a face back. I made another face. Soon we were both lying on her bedroom floor, laughing hysterically.

At midnight, everyone gathered around the TV in the living room to watch the ball drop in Times Square. A huge crimson neon *1989* lit up the New York night. Linda's friends began hugging and kissing each other and then they broke into a mangled version of "Auld Lang Syne." I hid in a corner, trying to find a way to disappear. Heather poked her head in. I picked her up and kissed her. Linda pushed her way through a clutch of people, hugged Heather, and pecked me on the cheek. She smiled hopefully. I carried Heather to her room and tucked her into her bed.

"Happy New Year, honey," I said, and kissed her.

"Happy New Year, Daddy," Heather said. She flung her arms around my neck. Her eyes lit up. "Mommy says you're moving back in with us."

I felt as if I'd been stabbed in the heart.

"Are you?"

"Well," I stammered. And then I mumbled, "I don't know. Maybe. We'll see."

Heather smiled, curled into a ball, and wrapped her arms around her pillow.

"Good night, Daddy."

" 'Night, honey." I turned off her light and crept out of her room. I closed her door and walked toward the kitchen. Someone popped open a bottle of champagne. People applauded. A mountain of foam rose over the top of the bubbly and gushed over the side of the bottle. It looked delicious. For a second, I wanted to grab the bottle and chug the whole thing down.

I took a deep breath and walked out of the room. I found Linda.

"I'm gonna go."

"What? Come on, it's early. The party's just warming up."

"I know . . . I'm just . . ."

She looked at me and her eyes glistened with drink and disappointment.

"Linda, it's different now. *I'm* different."

"I want us to be back together, Mark, the way it was. It was good, mostly, wasn't it?"

I lowered my head. I wanted to run. She picked my chin up with her hand.

"Wasn't it?"

I didn't know what to say. She staggered a little. Behind us, someone shrieked. Then there was a roar of laughter and a *bang* from another champagne bottle, this one loud as a gunshot.

"I'll call you," I said.

It was the only exit line I could think of.

The breakup just happened. I was talking to Linda on the phone, making arrangements to spend time with Heather over the weekend, and the words slipped out.

"Linda, I can't do this."

"What? Mark . . ."

"I can't do it anymore. It's not there for me. It's not *there*. We've grown so far apart, and we're going in such different directions. It's not your fault. It just would be better . . . look, I want a divorce."

There was a hole on the other end of the phone. I held on, waited for her to speak. A thousand thoughts flew through my mind.

Why hadn't I told her in person? Wouldn't that have been the decent thing to do? And my God, how is this going to affect Heather? I have to do this, though. I can't live like this anymore. I don't want to hurt Linda. And I am hurting her, can't help hurting her . . .

I could hear her crying. First soft, sad tears, then harsh bitter tears of rage. Then Heather was on the line and she was crying, too, and I heard her say in a muffled, pained voice, "I thought we were a family," and then the guilt rushed in and set itself in emotional stone and I pictured my former life with Linda, the innocent bystander, as I used her, used her to get a better deal from a judge so I could get probation instead of prison, used her to get a license to sell cars so I could work my scams, used her and used her and used her until I had used her up and the guilt hemorrhaged and burst and through all of it, I knew that it was wrong, Linda and I, it was all wrong, and I had to make my life right. I felt enormous essential pain. And no voluntary suffering. None.

And then it was done.

Linda and I filed for divorce. I settled into life with Harriet, working in the office, leading Friday night services, running two weekly Torah study groups, speaking all over the city, and studying and learning with Jonathan. My days were action-packed, which is why, I guess, I never saw it coming. I got blindsided. *Wham.* I should've seen it, though; I should've seen it.

I've always been a little out of step when it came to dating. In my defense, when I approached women, I was usually drunk or desperate. And before Linda I mainly dated barmaids and hookers. When I didn't pay for it, I was too drunk to care what I said. Booze made me bold. And stupid. I didn't care what my line was; I never thought about it. Half the time my rap worked and I got laid, and half the time I got the brush-off. It didn't bother me either way. I'd just keep on going like the Energizer Bunny. I'd make a phone call or pop the question at the bar: *Hey, honey, will you come home with me and for how much?*

That's why my relationship with Harriet was so confusing. I knew we were more than friends. And I knew how I felt about her. She shook me up in a way I'd never felt before in my life.

I was starting to go nuts. I was having all these thoughts and impulses and I'd almost do something, almost, and then I'd back off. I'd stand there, speechless, frozen like a statue. The woman made me sweat. Seriously. I actually got *warm* when I thought about her. And when I thought about doing something, making a move, I'd burn up.

After Linda and I split up, thoughts of Harriet began to pile up inside my brain. I couldn't get her out of my head. I had to do something. Had to act.

Finally, I decided on a plan.

I was going to ask her out on a date.

A movie. Simple. The classic first date. Of course, she'd have to drive. That was okay. She drove all the time. I had to get off the dime. I had see if we were ever going to take our relationship to the next level.

When though?

Timing is everything. I had to figure that out. I had to figure out the right time. I didn't want to rush anything, and didn't want to wait too long.

Then the second-guessing started.

Maybe I was reading the signs wrong. That was a definite possibility. Like I said, I don't know from signs. I know from *Here's a hundred bucks, thank you very much, don't let the door hit you on the way out.*

I began to think and plan. I started calculating the best time to make my move. Morning? On the way in to work? Nah. She's preoccupied. And if she says no, both our days are ruined and I look like a fool. How about lunch? I'll come by for lunch and casually ask her out for Saturday night. Maybe do it as a joke so if she turns me down, I can save face.

No. Lunch is no good. There are a million people around or some crisis to deal with and the phones are always ringing. It's too crazy.

Got it.

The way home. I'll ask her tonight in the car. I'll find the right moment. When we stop at a red light. Dumb. When she pulls up at my apartment. Perfect.

It was the end of January. Harriet wanted to leave Beit T'Shuvah a little earlier than usual. We were driving to my place. I was ready and I was nervous. I didn't say much on the way home. Come to think of it, neither did Harriet. Harriet pulled up in front of the halfway house. There was a small silence.

Now.

I started to ask her if she and—

Damn it! I'm warm again. Hot. Sweat is beading up on my brow, forming into a fucking pond. And my *mouth* . . . all of a sudden, my mouth is as dry as the desert.

I swallowed. Okay. Here goes.

"I have to tell you something, Mark," Harriet said. She was frowning. This was serious. She had bad news.

"What's the matter?"

"Are you all right? You're sweating."

"It's hot in here. I'll just crack a window."

"It's January. It's forty degrees out."

I forced a smile and plunged my palm into the ocean of sweat formerly known as my forehead.

"Here's the thing," Harriet said. She wasn't looking at me. She was gazing straight ahead at nothing. "I have a date tonight."

I blinked. "A *date*?"

"Yeah."

"With a guy?"

"Yes. I'm straight. In case you were wondering."

"No, I knew, I mean, I assumed . . . *tonight*?"

"In fact, in about an hour. I sort of have to get home—"

"Who is he?" Shit. I'd said that too fast. Too loud. I blew

my cool. I lowered my voice, went for casual, disinterest. "I'm curious, that's all."

"I don't know him. It's a blind date. My friend fixed us up. We're just going out for a drink."

We couldn't look at each other. We sat in the front seat of her car, the two of us, gazing dimly through her windshield. Neither of us spoke forever.

"Well, that's *terrific*," I said. "You should get out. Do you good. You work very hard. Need to relax. Have a social life. Absolutely. Why shouldn't you date?"

"Right. I mean . . . why not?"

"Right."

I tapped my finger on the dashboard, frowned again, pretended to peer at something important in the distance. There was nothing out there. I was buying time, trying to figure out what to say, what to do, trying to recover from the shock, from having blown my chance.

"Okay," I said. "Great. I'll see you tomorrow."

"Right."

"Have a, you know, have a, nice, time."

"Thanks. I mean, it's just for a drink."

"I don't drink," I said lamely, and squinted at her, waved, and got out of the car as fast as I could.

HARRIET

"That night was the beginning. The moment the relationship changed. Shifted. It went from an intense friendship, spiritual connection, soul mates, all of that, to something more, something romantic. There had been flirtations before. I was definitely starting to get interested."

A little girl look dances across Harriet's face. "I got home from the blind date, got out of the car, and Mark was sitting on my steps with a flower. A rose. It was nice. I don't remember what he said. I don't know if he said anything. We started making out. And as we were kissing, I heard a little voice in my head saying, Uh-oh, you're not going to move him in, you can't do that, don't move him in. Go slow."

She shrugs. "He moved in a few weeks later. What could I do? It was time for him to move out of the halfway house. We drove all over looking for apartments. It was tough. He had no credit and every apartment we saw was too expensive. I was determined that I was not going to pay his rent. I'd learned that lesson over time. Finally, I gave up and I just moved him in. Soul mates, roommates. What are you gonna do, right? It was scary. And there were times, oh yeah, there were times . . . and I still knew without question that it was the right move."

As soon as we moved in together, the roller-coaster ride began. Life with Harriet was hot and cold, easy and natural, soothing and insane. My head was spinning from all the changes we put each other through.

At the same time, Beit T'Shuvah started experiencing growing pains. We moved in more residents. We went from a low of ten people to a max of twenty-five. We were out of beds, out of space; we were bursting at the seams. We were sought out by a constant stream of rabbis, lawyers, doctors, parole officers, and scared and distraught parents. In the Jewish community, the issue of addiction is often swept under the rug. Beit T'Shuvah pushed this problem to the forefront and offered a possible solution. The Jewish community began to embrace us.

Then, suddenly, there was a flash point, a test for Beit T'Shuvah and for Harriet and me.

There was a guy who worked at Beit T'Shuvah. A former addict. Harriet had moved him up the ranks. He had become a high-level staff member with a ton of power and responsibility. He clearly saw me as a threat. He began to undermine everything I would say and do. I was getting a very bad vibe. I had to step back and sort out whether I was jealous of him or whether I just didn't trust him. I figured it out. I didn't trust him. Didn't trust him at all.

Harriet was defensive. "You have to give people the benefit of the doubt. You can't be so negative. He's gone through his shit. He's changed."

I didn't buy it. I've got too much street in me. Once a scam artist, always a scam artist. I should know. I'm still scamming. I'm just working a different side of the street now, that's all. I know who I am.

And I knew who this guy was. I told Harriet. She wouldn't listen. One thing about me then: I had to be right. And if you didn't listen to me, I became a gorilla. We started to get into it. It was clear as a bell to me: This guy wanted in on both Beit T'Shuvah and Harriet. I told her to watch out for him. She wouldn't see it. One night, it blew up.

"You're blind," I said. "You don't see what he's doing."

"What are *you* doing?"

"What do you mean?"

"Are you asking me to choose?"

"No," I said, lowering my voice to a whisper. The fury was bubbling up inside me. I was sick of this fight, sick of trying to make her see my point, sick of trying to be right. "You don't have to choose. I'm gonna choose. I choose to *FUCKING QUIT!*"

I stormed out of the room, nearly ripping the door off its hinges as I wound up and slammed it shut.

I went for a walk, a walk that lasted two hours. I wandered into a coffee shop, sat in a back booth, and swilled coffee until my hands were shaking. Then I went back to the apartment. Harriet was stretched out across the living room couch hiding in a book. She didn't look up as I came into the room. I planted myself in a chair and pretended to leaf through a magazine.

We didn't speak that night. The next morning as Harriet got ready to drive in to Beit T'Shuvah, I walked into the kitchen wearing my jogging suit. She stared at me.

"You're not dressed."

"I told you. I quit. I don't work for you anymore. I don't work at Beit T'Shuvah."

Harriet blinked, stumbled over her words. "What are you—?"

"I'll find a job. I'll pay my share of the rent, don't worry about it."

This time Harriet stormed out.

I took a job with a guy I knew from the joint selling lightweight, oversized workout pants. My customers were sporting goods stores I plucked out of the Yellow Pages. My showroom was the trunk of my car. As far as Beit T'Shuvah went, I couldn't let go entirely. I still led my weekly Torah study groups and ran Friday night services twice a month.

Harriet and I lived together in a state that was somewhere between mutual isolation and one-syllable conversation. The inside of our apartment had all the cozy warmth of an igloo. We weren't even angry anymore. We were stubborn. And sad.

We didn't want it to be like this. Yet we couldn't stop because neither of us could admit we were wrong.

Then a sportswear company in Japan came up with a line of workout pants that were more stylish, more lightweight, and much cheaper, and the company I worked for went belly-up. My friend immediately rolled me into another job that was even worse than selling pants out of my car: selling drill bits over the phone.

Every morning I got up at three-thirty and rode the bus downtown to a boiler room where I sold over the phone from 4 A.M. until 10 A.M.

This was a disaster.

I couldn't sell on the phone. Could not do it. I have to be face-to-face. Have to make eye contact. Have to be able to read my customer's face and find the sizzle.

I tried to make this work. I'd pick up the phone, dial a number, begin my pitch, and my mouth would go dry. I'd stumble over my spiel, say things out of order, retreat to the beginning.

"Let me start again, ma'am. I didn't mean to say *bill drits.* What I meant was . . . hello?"

I did this for a solid week. Squandered every hot lead. Squashed every follow-up. Then one day someone shouted across the room, "Mark, you got a call." I picked up the phone. It was Harriet.

"I'm sorry," she said.

"Me too," I said.

"You were right. He was full of shit. And he started using again. It's a mess."

I didn't say anything. I closed my eyes, tried to shut out the selling and swearing and shouting that was swirling all around me. I didn't care if I was right. I just wanted to get the hell out of there.

"Mark," Harriet said, "I need you."

"I need you, too."

"Come back."

"I will."

"When?"

"Is now too soon?"

"Not soon enough."

"Mark?"

"Yeah?"

"We can never do this again."

"We won't."

We never did.

W e were married on July 22, 1990, in our friend's back-yard in Woodland Hills in what was later confirmed as record-breaking heat.

It was a gangster wedding. My choice. Harriet wore a pearl-white dress. I wore a white suit and white felt hat. Arrangements of tulips, roses, and sunflowers burst from a lineup of bouquets that formed a bridal path through the center of the backyard. A keyboard player leaned into "My Way" as the guests arrived, then swung into a Rat Pack version of the "Wedding March" as Harriet and I strolled toward the chuppah—my *talis* held aloft by four friends—and three sweltering rabbis. Yes, *three*. Hers, mine, and ours. Hers was Rabbi Sue Ellwell, who volunteered at Beit T'Shuvah, ours was Jonathan Omer-man, and mine was, of course, Mel Silverman.

Once the ceremony started, a mixture of sweat and tears drizzled down my cheeks. Harriet and I faced each other and spoke the vows we had written. We wanted our marriage to have a *purpose*. That was crucial to us both. We were forming a covenant, which is more than a contract because a covenant involves God. Forming a covenant means that I don't serve Harriet and I don't serve myself. I serve and am loyal to and am committed to a new union called Harriet/Mark/God, and not necessarily in that order. God is part of this. Has to be. By including God, we are bound to create a relationship that is spiritual and nurturing. That's an automatic. And by making our agreement a covenant, we vowed to keep our marriage holy.

We told each other that we were committed to working things out, no matter what. Through our conversations and discussions and readings, especially Scott Peck's book *The Road Less Traveled,* we realized that love is not a feeling. Love is an act of will. Love is an action. It's not a momentary state of mind or a rush of blood to the head. That's lust. That goes away. When you accept that love is an act of will, you realize that you constantly have to work at it. It's the opposite of love that means never having to say you're sorry. Love means working your ass off and never giving up.

The rabbis pronounced us husband and wife. I stepped on a lightbulb wrapped in a napkin, kissed the bride, and mingled and ate a buffet brunch with a dozen of our closest friends. Harriet and I honeymooned at the Lawrence Welk Resort in Palm Springs, where, I was told, the temperature approached that of the surface of the sun. I don't know. We didn't spend that much time outside.

10

Rabbi Mark

ED

*Rabbi Ed Feinstein is squat and sturdy and bobs when he
moves, like a former point guard. He settles into a chair at the
center of the conference table in his office. Books are
everywhere—around him, over him, hovering like a flock of
beloved birds.*

*You notice then the light in the room. It circles his head like
a halo, as if Rabbi Ed Feinstein has been brushed by an angel. It
is possible. You feel something profound in his presence. You feel
energized, moved, inspired. Then Ed speaks. You are riveted by
his power and dazzled by his language. And you realize that Ed
Feinstein is more than a gifted storyteller.*

He is a poet.

I met Mark in the early 1990s. I was the director of Camp
Ramah, which was a big Jewish summer camp in Ojai,
California. Someone told me about this guy who had just gotten out of prison and was working in a rehab center that his
wife had set up. He was supposedly a real character. He had a
message, though, a strong message for kids. He was speaking
to them about addictions and criminal behavior, and he had a

lot to say about how to avoid making bad choices. Charismatic. That's the word people used.

I invited him up to the camp. At camp, kids aren't used to sitting quietly and listening to a lecture. You really had to grab their attention. Well, Mark came up, and, man, did he grab them. Grabbed them and held them in the palm of his hand for an hour. Mark would do a kind of rap. He spoke this language that I'd never really heard. Addiction is a hole in your soul. He was raw and crude and deeply passionate. After all, he was a kid just like the kids in front of him. He was a kid who went to synagogue, a kid who came from a good family, a kid who made bad choices and went very wrong. He was very compelling. He got to those kids. And he got to me.

We spoke and we connected. He started coming to Saturday morning services at Valley Beth Shalom, where I was a rabbi. Beit T'Shuvah only had services Friday nights so he came here to try us out. That's when I discovered his brilliance when it came to interpreting the text. He came to Torah from a whole different place, a perspective I had not seen. I found that out during services.

As part of the morning service, we spend about an hour studying the weekly Torah portion. We do it in dialogue. I stand up in front of the congregation and I ask questions. We go back and forth. I was stunned at the quality of Mark's answers. The depth was remarkable. He would turn a discussion from something external to something internal, something personal. We had a bright group here Saturday mornings—writers, lawyers, doctors, some really bright people. Mark had incredible insight. It was all from his life. From the school of hard knocks. It wasn't the way I was trained. My training comes from books. Mark's training came from the street.

Here's one example. The central narrative of the Hebrew

Bible is the escape from slavery. It's the most powerful event. Everything leads up to it. Mark would schlep us—three hundred people in the congregation—to the question of Are you a slave? And how do you know? What if you're a slave and you don't know it? To what are you a slave? Egypt is not a place in the Middle East, he'd say. Egypt is a place in your soul. It is those things that you are attached to that rule you instead of you ruling them, instead of allowing God to rule you. It was stunning. And very deep.

For Mark, Passover is the holiday. You'd think it would be Yom Kippur because it's all about T'Shuvah. It's not. His holiday is Passover because it's all about the great struggle to escape from slavery and that the journey takes forty years across the desert. You don't just go out of Egypt right into the Promised Land. It's a struggle. You watch those people at Beit T'Shuvah. You look at Mark. You don't just jump out of an addiction, clean yourself up, and go, "Hey, everybody, I'm clean!" It's a long, hard journey. A struggle. Mark would talk about that all the time. He'd say, "You're a slave! You don't even know it!" He'd scream at this group of suburban Jews, "Who's your Pharaoh?" It's a profound lesson.

I fell in love with him. I would offer the narrative, the stories, the questions. Questions like, Why make Moses mute? That's an interesting character choice. Why make the greatest prophet of our time mute?

Mark would go a level deeper. Mark wanted to know, Who is the mute prophet in you? What is it that your silence won't let you speak?

He got to me. Shabbos after Shabbos. He didn't know how to read the book. Couldn't read the Hebrew. I knew the Hebrew, knew the history, knew the Midrash, knew the

Talmud. He needed me to help him read the book. I needed him to show me this new, dynamic way to interpret it.

One week, after services, we started learning together. Every week. It was a kind of symbiosis and a revelation to us both. That was, what, ten years ago? We're still going.

Around the time I began studying with Ed, Beit T'Shuvah joined with Gateways Hospital and opened an outpatient clinic in Santa Monica. The partnership instantly gave us more credibility and more visibility. It also gave me a new boss.

She ran Gateways's clinical programming arm and she wanted to meet me. One day, I got into my new car (a used Toyota) and drove a half-hour from downtown L.A. to Santa Monica. (Yes, I finally got my license!)

Her office was down a dim hallway, last room on the right. The door was open. I walked into a tight, sterile, angular room. My boss sat behind a metal desk. It was mid-afternoon. The day was starting to lose the light, and she had her shades drawn.

I smiled. She didn't. She didn't even offer me a chair. She craned her neck at me.

"I have a problem with you leading groups," she said.

I scratched my beard. "What's the problem?"

She pulled her chair deeper into shadows and swiveled farther away from me.

"You don't even have a college degree."

"That's true," I said. "So what?"

"How do I know that you're qualified?"

"I'm qualified because I know what I'm doing."

She held up her hand. "Mr. Borovitz, it's very difficult for

me to talk to you because I don't know what you *know*.
We don't have a common denominator. A college degree is a
minimum—"

"*Awfully* nice meeting you," I said.

I bolted the hell out of there before I said something I
would regret.

I hated that conversation because it was insulting and humil-
iating. And it was true. I did know what I was doing, and I
did need a college degree. I knew I had to go back to school.
The one thing I wouldn't do, though, was give up my groups
and my Torah study sessions and my counseling and my outreach. In other words, I wasn't giving up my day job.

I heard about a college, National University, that was
geared toward people like me—working people who wanted
to complete a college degree at night, on weekends, and during
summers. I sat at the kitchen table one night and flipped
through the catalogue. I let out a half-sigh, half-laugh. I mean,
shit, I was forty-two years old and I was thinking about going
back to *school*? I glanced over at Harriet. She was curled up on
the couch, lost in a philosophical novel by some European
egghead. In a second I'd join her with a copy of this week's
Sporting News. What a pair we were. She liked the college idea
a lot.

"The degree will give you more credibility," she said. "It
can't hurt Beit T'Shuvah's credibility, either."

I could see her point. Right now, I was just a crazy ex-con
college dropout with a message. I could imagine some of the
kids I spoke to saying, "Should we believe him? He never
even finished college. How smart is he?"

I decided to go for it.

I busted my ass and graduated from National in 1995.

Not bad.

It only took me twenty-eight years to get through college.

ED

In 1993, I had colon cancer.

I had surgery and a year of chemotherapy. My doctor told me there was a good chance the cancer would go away. They monitored me carefully. Three years went by, and it looked like he was right. Then four years later, Thanksgiving 1997, my doctor called me in a panic. "Ed, I need you to come in right now."

One of my tests had come back positive. They tested me again and discovered that I had a tumor in my liver. A tumor in the liver is usually fatal. At the least, the surgery is extremely dangerous. They gave me a very small chance of surviving.

I was very frightened. I went in for a huge surgery. Ten hours. I came out of the operating room Monday night. Tuesday I was so drugged, I was out cold all day.

Wednesday I wake up; it must have been four-thirty, five in the morning. I'm hooked up to a hundred tubes and catheters. I had four IVs going. I'm in extreme pain. My mother had spent the night in the hospital with me. My wife had gone home. I wake up, I can barely see, everything is blurry, it's 5 A.M. and there's this massive figure at my bedside.

Borovitz.

He just . . . showed up. I don't believe this. Is it a dream? He's standing there, five o'clock in the morning, grinning at me.

"So," he says, "how you feeling?"

"I feel like shit."

"Good! I brought books."

I look at him. "You brought books?"

"Yep. We're gonna learn."

"What do you mean, we're gonna learn? I can't see the page."

"I'll read, you explain."

I'd had ten hours of surgery, I was doped up, tubed up, lying in a hospital bed in a complete daze and Borovitz is standing there at my bedside, Cheshire cat grin on his face, with books. He wants to learn.

It was such a profound idea.

You are alive; you have to learn.

That is what we do.

And it was his way of saying to me, I'm not letting you die.

So he read and I talked. He came back the next day. And the next. Every day at five o'clock in the morning, for two weeks, he came with books.

And we learned together. Slowly my eyesight came back and I could focus on a page. We sat together every morning for an hour. My mother couldn't believe it. The first day she said, "Who the hell are you?"

"Borovitz."

"Oh," she said. "I heard about you."

He came every single morning. I was so frightened. They gave me such a small chance of surviving. And Borovitz wouldn't let me go. Gradually, I got stronger. Got out of the hospital. They didn't think I would live. It's going on six years now. Every morning he sat at my bedside and we learned.

When I talk to people about Mark Borovitz and I say he is the Holy Thief who steals souls back from the devil and steals souls back from the dead ... I'm one of them.

I'm one of them.

Okay. Got the college degree. Next step . . . a master's in marriage and family counseling, right? That's what the next step felt like, anyway. That's what I was doing every day at Beit T'Shuvah, counseling people. What the hell. Might as well stay in school.

I took a month off and enrolled in a couple of graduate courses at National. After the very first class, I knew it wasn't right. I couldn't relate to what I was being taught. It felt as if I were walking backward. I felt inauthentic. Fake. What I was doing at Beit T'Shuvah was spiritual counseling. This was . . . I didn't really know what it was. I just knew it wasn't me. So I quit. Dropped out.

Then one day, Harriet read an article in the *Jewish Journal* that announced the opening of the Zeigler School of Rabbinic Studies at the University of Judaism. She didn't even look up from the paper.

"You know what?" she said. "You should be a rabbi."

My response was profound and articulate.

"Huh?"

That night I had dinner with Ed Feinstein. He'd been uncharacteristically quiet the whole evening. He stared at his salad, which he'd been pushing around with his fork for the last fifteen minutes.

"I've been thinking," he said. "You should apply to rabbinical school. You need the stamp. You're acting like a rabbi anyway. Make it official."

"Have you been talking to Harriet?"

"No, why?"

"She said this same thing this morning."

"Smart woman," Ed said. "Look, in order for your message to be really heard, you have to have *Rabbi* in front of your

name. It's that simple. Right now you're preaching the tradition, you're teaching it, and people are listening to you. I mean,
who wouldn't listen to you? You're right up in their face. The
point is, they'll listen even more if you are a rabbi. Rabbi Mark
Borovitz carries more weight than Mark Borovitz, loud, charismatic, caring ex-con."

"You and Harriet are working a double team. Nice. My
wife and my best friend."

"I'm telling you, I have not spoken to Harriet."

"If that's true, you're both crazy."

"Why?"

"Me? A rabbi? It's . . . *crazy.*"

"Your whole life's been crazy. Might as well keep the insanity going."

He had me there. I shook my head. Ed smiled at me like a
poker player with the winning hand.

"Rabbi Mark Borovitz," I said, trying it out.

"Got a nice ring to it," Ed said.

In the deepest part of me, in my heart and in my soul, I
knew that I was meant to be a rabbi.

Harriet and Ed were right. I was already acting like a rabbi
both at Beit T'Shuvah and in the community. Granted, I was a
different kind of rabbi. I taught and lectured as much from my
life as from the Torah. I couldn't see myself as only a congregational rabbi. I saw myself as a personal rabbi, one who made
house calls. Or court calls. Or prison calls. I'd go wherever
Jews were in need, in trouble with drugs or booze or the law. I
wanted to help anyone who was lost find his or her way. The
problem for me wasn't being a rabbi. The problem was *becoming* a rabbi.

I decided to drive to Venice Beach and take a long walk to clear my head. It was late afternoon when I got to the boardwalk. I stuffed my hands into the pockets of my jogging suit and strolled among the skateboarders, rollerbladers, street performers, sidewalk vendors, tourists, and homeless people. I watched the sun slowly morph into an orange ball the color of the jumpsuit I wore in prison. Then I closed my eyes and pictured myself in rabbinical school.

Four years.

Minimum.

That would be the commitment. Four *years.*

I was forty-four years old. I wouldn't be an ordained rabbi until I was almost fifty . . .

Starting a brand-new life at fifty.

I wagged my head from side to side, trying that on.

I didn't mind it. In fact, after what I'd been through, fifty seemed young. A rabbi needs wisdom. Life experience. I had that in spades.

Then I pictured myself sitting in a classroom, six hours a day, four and a half days a week. Concentrating during lectures, taking notes, studying, doing homework, writing term papers, wading through research. Grad school. Structure, structure, structure.

I hate structure.

I have trouble sitting still for five minutes. When Ed and I study together, I'm all over the place. I sit down, I get up, I pace, I prowl, I sit back down, I jump up, I kick the chair out, I shout, I walk . . . I cannot sit still.

How would I sit still for four years?

Toughest of all, I'd have to learn Hebrew.

Have you ever taken a good look at Hebrew? We're not

talking about a foreign language that uses English letters. We're talking about an ancient alphabet, a mishmash of scratches, lines, dots, and curlicues that, by the way, you read from *right* to *left*. And the sound of the language is a garble of weird guttural tones that resemble an asthmatic old guy clearing his throat. That's Hebrew.

Sure, I know a lot of Hebrew prayers. Knowing Hebrew prayers is one thing. Learning how to read, understand, and *speak* Hebrew is a whole new ball game.

There's no way around it. To become a rabbi, you have to be able to read and interpret the ancient texts. You have to be fluent in Hebrew. It's a requirement.

The night air turned cold. I ducked my head into my collar and kept walking. I blinked at the moon, a silver sliver off to my left, and I imagined myself hunched over an ancient dusty volume, my finger pointed at a mass of indecipherable scrawl. I'm desperately trying to plow through the lines, fumbling for some meaning, some understanding, some light . . .

I strained to visualize myself conquering the language of my ancestors, tried to imagine Hebrew flying off my tongue.

All I saw was a blank slide.

I turned back. It was getting late. Harriet was probably starting to worry. I passed three guys huddled around a small fire they'd made in a garbage can. One of them played a brutal version of "Strangers in the Night" on a banged-up violin. I laid a five-dollar bill into a Dodger cap lying upside down at his feet. He waved a thank-you with his bow.

I slipped behind the wheel of my car and headed toward the 405 freeway. It was dark, a couple hours after rush hour, and traffic was light. It would only take me twenty minutes to get home. I steered easily with my left hand, flipped on a jazz station. Brubeck's "Take Five" tinkled through my Bose system. I decided to pretend that I had been accepted into rabbinical school. What would a typical day be like?

For one thing, I'd still be working at Beit T'Shuvah full-time, or as many hours as I could. I'd have to in order to afford the tuition. I'd work early in the mornings and late afternoons, and on the weekends. I'd go to school from nine to three, Monday through Thursday, from nine to one on Fridays. I'd study and do my homework . . . when? I guess from eight at night until I finished. And I'd sleep . . .? Okay, so I wouldn't sleep for four years.

When I got home, Harriet was warming something in the oven for my dinner. I thanked her, pulled it out, and started nibbling. I told her where I'd been and what I'd been thinking. I went through my thought process, step-by-step. When I was done, she paused. "Look, Mark, nobody's going to force you to become a rabbi. It's your choice. You have to want it."

"I know," I said.

I didn't look up from my dinner.

"Harriet," I said, "I want it."

I did want to be a rabbi. Wanted it more than anything. Wanted it because I knew that's who I was. I knew it was my calling. I knew that I needed to go to rabbinical school.

And I was afraid.

I was afraid that I wouldn't get in.

So to protect myself from this fear, I didn't apply.

Every night before I went to bed I stared at the Zeigler School of Rabbinic Studies application packet. Read it through, then pushed it aside and promised myself I'd fill it out another day when I was fresh, when I had more time, when I was more focused. I never did. One morning I woke up, rolled out of bed, and peered at the calendar. It was a Thursday in mid-January and I realized that my application was due . . . *tomorrow.*

It was the moment of truth.

I walked into the bathroom and stared at myself in the mirror and I whispered, "Okay, pal, tell me the truth. Who are you?"

I answered back, "Rabbi Mark Borovitz."

I showered, got dressed, stuffed the application packet into my briefcase, and raced over to Valley Beth Shalom Synagogue. I charged into Ed Feinstein's office.

"Okay," I shouted. "I'll do it."

I dumped everything on his desk.

Ed said, "What is this?"

"Everything. The application. The forms. All of it. You fill it out, I'll go."

"You know what you're in for, right?"

"Hurry up before I change my mind."

"You have to write the essay."

"Fine, I'll write the essay. The other stuff, the nuts-and-bolts application shit, I ain't doing."

"You're insane, you know that?"

"What, applying to rabbinical school at the age of forty-four with a rap sheet longer than Capone's? You call that insane?"

Ed mumbled, "He's a maniac."

He leaned over and kissed me on the top of my head. "Have a seat, *meshuggener.* This is gonna take a while."

Ed booted up his computer, typed out my application, and wrote an unbelievable letter of recommendation. Meanwhile, I grabbed a pen and blasted through the personal essay. Ed polished off all the paperwork, then got on the phone, called

Jonathan and Mel, and told them he needed letters of recommendation. He faxed them the forms, hopped in his car, and
picked those up. By the time he got back, I was polishing the
last paragraph of the essay. I handed it to him. He stuffed that
and everything else into the envelope. I grabbed the packet,
raced over to the rabbinical school, and hand delivered it five
minutes before the deadline.

It was done. On time. Somehow. Thanks to Ed.

And then came the hardest part.

The waiting.

I tried to escape into work, tried not to think about getting
in. It didn't work. I thought about it every moment of every
day.

I started getting calls of support and encouragement. Mel
Silverman called. And Jonathan Omer-man. My mother. My
brother Neal and my sister, Sheri, who both now lived in
New Jersey, and my brother Stuart, who had moved back to
Cleveland to better accommodate his battle with MS. I heard
from people from my past, names I vaguely remembered and
voices I thought I'd never hear again.

Heather called often. We started getting closer. The famil-
iarity and fun were slowly seeping back into our conversations.

"What are the odds of you getting in?" she asked me one
day.

"Long," I said. "I'm not exactly rabbi material."

"They'd be crazy not to let you in," Heather said.

"Well, thanks."

"Hey, Dad," she said. "You become a rabbi, maybe I'll
study for my bat mitzvah with you."

"That would be something," I said. "That would really be
something."

"I'm holding a good thought."

"Me, too."

It was a Friday afternoon. I was going nuts at work. I decided to leave Beit T'Shuvah early. I took off around noon and headed home to the Valley. I made myself some lunch, flicked on CNN, couldn't concentrate on a word the newscaster was saying, turned off the set, and read the sports section for the third time that day. Then I heard a *thunk* outside my front door.

The mail.

I knew it had come. The envelope.

The answer.

I couldn't move. I was frozen. My whole body clenched. I forced myself to my feet and started to walk. My legs felt leaden and far away. I finally opened the front door.

I saw the envelope right away. It was lying across a couple of magazines and a stack of bills. I scooped it up and went back into the house. I was so nervous that I left the rest of the mail outside.

I held the envelope in my hand. I turned it over. Squeezed it. Held it up to the light. I brushed the envelope lightly against the side of my face. I slapped it against my thigh.

What I didn't do was open it.

I sat at the kitchen table and placed the envelope in front of me. I stared at it. And stared. I reached over for the phone and called Harriet.

"It's here," I said.

She gasped. "What does it say? No, wait, is the envelope thick or thin?"

I picked it up, pressed it, let it rest in my hand, measured it, weighed it.

"I don't know."

"It has to be either thick or thin."

"It's not. It's both. Not too thick and not that thin."

"Never mind." She sucked in a roomful of air and exhaled deeply. I could almost feel her breath against my cheek through the phone. "Okay. What does it say?"

"I don't know."

"What do you mean?"

"I haven't opened it."

"Open it!"

"I can't."

She paused.

"We're going to open it together. Okay? I'm with you. Ready?"

I nodded.

"Mark?"

"I'm here."

I stuck a finger inside the envelope and slowly, oh so slowly, ripped off the top. I peered inside. I couldn't see anything. I reached in and pulled out a letter. I started to unfold it and stopped because I was trembling.

"There's a letter."

"Read it."

I closed my eyes, then opened them narrowly and began to read the first sentence. "It says . . . mazel tov."

"Mazel . . . MARK! Oh my God!"

"I got in."

Harriet screamed. I heard other voices, other people screaming, shouting, and applause.

"Come here," Harriet said. "Bring the letter."

"I'll be right there."

I folded the letter and slid it back into the envelope. I got into the car and headed back to Beit T'Shuvah, the House of Return. As I drove, the faces of my life flashed in my mind's eye. First, I saw Harriet. She was beaming. Then I saw Ed and Mel and Jonathan. I saw my uncle Harry, my aunt Nettie, and my uncle Marty. I saw my mother. She was crying. I saw my grandparents. I saw my brothers and my sister. I saw Heather. She was laughing. I saw Linda. And Mario. I saw Charlie. I saw myself at thirteen. I was standing in front of the congregation at the Heights Temple. Hebrew prayers danced off my lips. And then I saw my father. He was smiling.

I drove downtown and turned left toward Beit T'Shuvah. All the residents and staff stood in the street. They saw me and they started waving and cheering. I drifted to a stop and they surrounded the car. Harriet flung open the door and practically pulled me out of the car. She threw her arms around my neck and hugged me and kissed me, and she wouldn't let go. She pulled away and looked at me through eyes that were moist and filled with pride and she kissed me again. Everyone applauded.

And then it hit me.

This wasn't my moment. This moment was for every misfit who felt he didn't belong and every outcast who was searching for her place. This moment was for all of us at Beit T'Shuvah.

Finally, we'd all been accepted.

I attended rabbinical school from June 1996 through May 2000. I spent six months in Israel by myself, where, exposed to Hebrew every waking moment of every day, I managed to master the language. Rabbinical school was challenging, stressful, and exhilarating. I complained often. Well okay, I complained *constantly* to Harriet and Ed. I hollered at them, "You two got me into this, you better get me through it!"

And they did. With good humor and immeasurable patience. I couldn't have done it without them.

Right before I was ordained, Beit T'Shuvah moved from our dilapidated house downtown to our newly remodeled building in West Los Angeles. It was the culmination of a dream, Harriet's dream, and mine, and a lot of other people's. It's wonderful to have this facility, which houses over one hundred residents. And I'm saddened that there is such a need to have a place like Beit T'Shuvah. And I'm sad because we're always full. There are so many lost and tortured souls, all seeking to find paths out of their own personal deserts, their own private wastelands. They know, at least, that I'm here for them. I'm always here.

I'm their rabbi.

11

Prophet

I believe that every life is worth fighting for. Every life, no matter how lost or battered, can change. Every life can live in the pure essence of one's soul. Every soul can heal. Every one.

NEAL

A few years ago, a man came up to me and asked, "Rabbi Neal Borovitz? Are you Mark Borovitz's brother?"

I said, "Yes."

He said, "Your brother saved my son's life."

Mark epitomizes a sermon I give. We're called Israel, not Shalomael. Interesting because shalom is the most important word in the Hebrew language. If we were Shalomael, it would mean that we were at peace with God. That's not who we are. We wrestle with God.

That's the essence of Judaism and the essence of my brother. Mark is a wrestler, and God is in the wrestling. And he won't quit. He can't do it. Doesn't know how. He takes on impossible challenges. He will not give up on people even if they've given up on themselves.

He called out of the blue. He asked for me. I was away, so he spoke to one of our social workers. He wanted to cut a deal. When I got back, I called the judge and got her to give him alternative sentencing while he waited for his trial to come up. I arranged to see him the next day.

He looked the same. A little older, a little wider across the middle, a little more used up. His Bronx accent was still thick as an egg cream.

"Mark," he said, "look at you."

"Charlie," I said.

We stood in the hallway outside my office. We hugged silently. We pulled apart and stared into each other's eyes.

"Been a while," I said.

Charlie Stein nodded, running his palm through his thinning silver hair.

"I've changed," Charlie said.

"Good."

"Really. I have. I gave up drinking. Coke, too."

"Seriously?"

"Seriously."

"I could use a good counselor," I said.

"What is this? You offering me a handout?"

"I'm offering you a *job*. You have to get your CDAC license. I can give you the hours."

"I'll get the license. That's not a problem."

Charlie coughed, a sudden hack. Then he teetered for a moment and pressed his palm against the wall for balance. He started to say something, then clamped his lips together.

"You all right?" I asked.

"I've got this trial. I think about it, it gets to me, that's all." Charlie lowered his head. "Mark . . . I'm a little pressed for cash."

"Can you start work tomorrow?"

He looked up. "I can start today."

"You're in luck." I reached for my wallet. "I pay in advance."

C harlie kept his word. In a matter of months, he received his Certified Drug and Alcohol Counselor's license. He led two groups at Beit T'Shuvah and was beloved by the residents. He had made a big change, and he was trying to give something back.

One day he didn't show up. I took over his group. Ten minutes after group ended, he called me on the phone.

"I'm sorry," Charlie said.

"Where are you?"

"I split. The trial came up."

"Charlie, you can't run away. You have to come back."

"I can't."

"You have to. They're gonna come looking for you. You have to turn yourself in."

His voice cracked. "You don't understand."

"Tell me where you are."

He hung up.

T he cops came that afternoon. Two round Irish detectives in matching powder blue suits. McEwing and Dunn.

McEwing swiped his nose with the back of his hand. "Your friend made a deal. Alternative sentence here for a plea."

"Now he took off," Dunn said as if I didn't know.

"Like breaking parole," McEwing said.

"I don't know what to tell you," I said. "I tried to talk to him. He won't come in."

McEwing swiped his nose again. "Nothing worse than a summer cold." He twisted his neck toward me. "We heard about you. Heard about this place. What you do here."

Dunn nodded, took in my cluttered office. The air conditioner had died that morning. My office felt like the inside of a pizza oven. "Lieutenant told us we don't come back with your boy, we have to arrest you for harboring a fugitive."

"That's bullshit," I said.

McEwing and Dunn laughed.

"A rabbi who curses," Dunn said.

"Well, I'm a little different."

"We heard that, too," said Dunn.

"Do you know where he is?" McEwing asked.

"I wish I did."

The two detectives stood up at the same time.

"You booking me?" I asked.

"The lieutenant don't know shit," Dunn said. "We told him we'd quit before we'd arrest you."

McEwing flipped a business card onto my desk. "He calls, you'll get in touch, right?"

"Yes."

"You do a good thing here," McEwing said.

Dunn said, "You might do even better if you had air conditioning."

Charlie dodged the police for nearly a year. In December, Dunn and McEwing responded to an anonymous phone tip and arrested him in a motel room. By then,

Charlie's rapidly advancing lung cancer had ravaged his body. He agreed to testify in return for a minimal sentence. He was granted compassionate release, and his brother checked him into a hospice. The doctor said that he had only a short time to live, maybe a matter of hours. I went to see him.

He was lying on a bed between five or six other beds. He had lost seventy pounds, and his face was folded into two deep dark crevices. His voice was breathy and soft and his hands were bony and frail. As I approached the bed, he looked at me without any recognition.

"Charlie," I said, "it's Mark."

He stared at me. His eyes clouded over. He reached out and grabbed my hand and squeezed. It felt as if I were being held in the grip of a child.

"Get me out of here," he said.

"Charlie . . ."

He blinked and dropped his head lightly onto his pillow. He peered at the ceiling. He began to pant, as if he'd just finished a run. "Mark?"

"Yes?"

"I was sick. I couldn't face the D.A."

"It's okay." I paused. "Charlie, you don't have to fight anymore. You can let go."

He started to cry. He gripped my hand harder. "Mark, I want to die clean."

"You are clean. You've done *T'shuvah.*"

And then Charlie smiled. "Who would've believed this? You . . . my rabbi."

"I know."

"The shit we pulled."

He started to cough. I reached over for a tissue and handed it to him. He shook his head. He didn't want to let go of my hand. He looked at me then, stared into my eyes, held me there for so long I wasn't sure if he'd stopped breathing. Finally, he said, "Rabbi Mark?"

"Yes."

"Please forgive me."

He slumped back into the bed. I closed my eyes and whispered a prayer. After a few minutes, I stood up. I leaned over and kissed him on the forehead.

"Good-bye, Charlie," I said.

I left. Charlie died two hours later.

I've spent a lot of time swimming upstream. Sixteen years ago, I decided to change direction. I saw that God had the river flowing a different way and I said, "I'm gonna go along with God's flow now. Not mine. Not yours. Too many times I went your way or mine and ended up underwater, almost drowning."

It's extremely tough to change direction in the middle of a raging river.

It's even tougher if you don't.

My brother Stuart died on January 16, 2001, in Cleveland, of complications from MS. He was fifty-five years old. According to the Jewish calendar, he died thirty-five years to the day that my father died.

Stuart was a kind, good man, who came into his own the closer he came to death. He spent many of the last years of his life getting around in a motorized wheelchair. He drove it himself, everywhere he could. He lived a life of grace and dignity and surprising independence. He was an inspiration.

I dedicate my life now to raising myself and others up. And in everything I do, like my brother Stuart, I give you the best that I have.

That's all I got, babe. That's all I got.

ED

There is a character in the Jewish faith called a prophet. The difference between a rabbi and a prophet is that a prophet doesn't ask to be a prophet. A prophet doesn't study to be a prophet. As Borovitz said to me, "Ed, a prophet gets to be called a prophet. He carries a message and it's there, something compelling, something burning, that he can't get out of him. Like Jeremiah. He talks about a fire in his belly that he can't extinguish."

In so many ways, Mark is more a prophet than a rabbi.

He was called to this. And there's this passion that he can't let go of. It dominates him. That's why he gets so volcanic.

Problem is, there isn't much of a market for prophets these days. A prophet is a terribly lonely person. He doesn't have a community. He doesn't have rabbis of past generations with whom he can share experiences. A rabbi does.

That's why I wanted Mark to become a rabbi. I wanted him to have a community of other scholars. I wanted him to meet and become familiar with other guys in Jewish history who had similar experiences. The only way to do that was to have him devote four years of his life, four solid years, to study. He did.

Now he's got the books and the history and the language and the community. And, like it or not, they've got him.

Mark evokes all these wonderful images from the Bible. Jonah and the whale. Joseph in the pit. The guy going as low as he can go. A guy getting as far away from the truth of his life as he possibly could. There is something about that image, even in science, something about hitting the apogee. You have to get to the absolute farthest point to see the truth of your life. You have to get that close to the devil to know that God exists.

It's still choppy. Choppy and jerky and messy. Not smooth. Never smooth. Life is not smooth for Mark. It's a bumpy ride. Bumpy, bumpy, bumpy. And it always will be.

That's the way it is for prophets.

Afterword

Beit T'Shuvah is a rehabilitation center, a congregation, a community, and a state of mind in which we explode the stereotypes of our culture. I have learned through time and experience that addiction is an equal opportunity disease, paying no notice to one's college degree, family name, home address, or bank account. Anyone can become an addict.

Rabbi Abraham Joshua Heschel said that each of us has a song inside us, received from God at our creation. Beit T'Shuvah helps people find and sing their own song and discover and live their unique purpose. We expose the lie that people cannot change. People do change.

Beit T'Shuvah attracts a cross section of society, from street people to Hollywood moguls and CEOs of major corporations. All are united in the search for truth, meaning, purpose, and freedom. We continue to serve the original mission of Beit T'Shuvah: to provide a place for people seeking to recover their authentic selves regardless of how much they can afford to pay for help.

Beit T'Shuvah, the House of Return and New Responses, offers programs, professional care, spiritual guidance, a home for anyone afflicted with the disease of addiction, and sanctuary for everyone who feels lost and empty. We are a community that opens our hearts to all who come through our doors.

We can be reached at www.beittshuvahla.org, rabbi@
beittshuvahla.org., and 310-204-5200.

Harriet and I thank God and the many people who have
helped us find and sing our song. May God bless all of you
with joy, love, and wholeness.

Acknowledgments

MARK

To all those whom I have harmed, I am deeply sorry, and I am living a life of decency and honor. I humbly ask for your forgiveness.

I want to acknowledge the chain of people who have made this book and my life possible. Blair Belcher, my friend, student, teacher, and agent, has believed in me since we met. Blair teaches me how to grow each day. Without her, this book never would have been written. She introduced me to one of my best study partners, Howard Sanders. Howie is also my agent, teacher, and friend. Howie and I study on Fridays and learn together how to be better men, husbands, friends, and humans. Howie introduced me to Alan Eisenstock, my partner in writing this book. Blair also introduced me to Caitlin Scanlon, who has urged me on to do this project and shows me how to live life to the fullest. Thank you Blair, Howie, and Caitlin for living my teachings.

Alan Eisenstock was initially reluctant to do this project with me. We have spent two and a half years absorbed in each other's lives. Alan really got me! He intuitively knew what questions to ask, how to give life to my memory. He has become my alter ego. We have lived this project with integrity and passion. It is so hard to describe all of my feelings, and I know that Alan knows how important a part of my life he has become. Thank you, Alan, for your love, commitment, and devotion and for always remembering that the covenant that we made was what has to be served. Thank you for caring enough to get to know my soul and allowing me to know yours.

Agent Wendy Sherman (imagine a rabbi with three agents) has believed in and pushed this project since she heard about it. Wendy is the consummate book agent, and a great person. Our relationship is the best mix of business and personal. Thank you for holding my hand through this process and for teaching me about another segment of life.

Thank you to Mauro DiPreta and Suzanne Balaban at William Morrow for believing in this project and for your belief in the possibility of change and your ability to recognize people who have changed. Your faith in me and in Alan made this a much richer experience. Thank you for joining our group of supporters of change. Thanks also to Joelle Yudin, Mauro's assistant, and to our transcriber, Ben Winters.

How do I thank Mel Silverman for restoring me to life? He held on to me when I was spiritually dead and breathed life into me. Mel is my teacher, my wise elder, my friend, and my colleague. Mel, thank you for my life and for all of the kind and loving words you spoke in this book. Rabbi Jonathon Omer-man was my spiritual guide during my first years out of prison. Jonathon taught me how to live without needing to be perfect. Thank you, Jonathon, for guiding me.

Rabbi Ed Feinstein is my best friend, my teacher, my colleague. Ed has been my "main man" for more than ten years. He knows me and loves me. I know him and love him. We have faced illness together and we have enjoyed life together. Ed, your words blow me away. Thank you for being you, for being the Holy Soul and great spirit that you are.

To my family: my mother, Millie; my sister, Sheri; and my brother, Neal. It has been a wild ride. They have lived this book with me, both during the writing of it and, more important, as the events described in it unfolded. Mom, I am truly sorry for the suffering that I caused you. Sheri, I am sorry for not being the brother that you needed. Neal, I am sorry that I caused you so much grief and worry, making you wonder when you would get a call that I was dead. Mom, thank you for sticking with me and loving me. Sheri, your devotion and love has sustained me. Neal, we speak five times a week. You consistently help me with any and all life issues. You are one of my biggest cheerleaders! Thanks so much.

I want to thank the past, present, and future residents of Beit T'Shuvah. You have all taught me so much and I am made small by your kindnesses. To the Board of Beit T'Shuvah, you have supported the mission, the dream, and Harriet and me. Without you, I would not be able to do what I do so well.

It is very difficult to explain how much I owe my father, Jerry. He has been a guiding light in my life, even when I didn't follow it. Dad, thank you for your spirit. You were not here long enough in years, but your teachings and spirit have inspired and saved many souls.

My daughter, Heather, is my hero. She has taught me how to believe in people even when they are not believable. Heather, you are my love. I could not live without you.

Harriet, my wife, my partner, my lover, my friend, you really have given me the gift of living well. You saw a diamond in the rough—very rough—and you have helped me polish and grow my soul. You inspire me each day to live fully and in the present. You push me to continue to grow and learn and help me to stay right-sized. You are my Eishet Hayil, my Woman of Valor. As Proverbs says, I am made great because of you and by you.

ALAN

This book could not have been written without the encouragement, wisdom, and participation of a loving community of supporters. They include:

Our families: Bobbie Eisenstock, Jonah Eisenstock, and Kiva Eisenstock; Harriet Rossetto, Heather Borovitz, Millie Borovitz, Neal Borovitz, and Sheri Borovitz-Linda.

Our teachers: Rabbi Ed Feinstein, Rabbi Mel Silverman, and Rabbi Jonathon Omer-man.

Our guides: Special Agent Wendy Sherman, Howie Sanders, Blair Belcher, and Caitlin Scanlon.

Our literary mavens: Mauro DiPreta (a gift of an editor), Suzanne Balaban, Joelle Yudin, and Ben Winters.

My muse: David Ritz. You got it rolling with three words: "Go to Cleveland."

And Shirley and Jim Eisenstock, Madeline and Phil Schwarzman, Susan Baskin and Richard Gerwitz, Susan Pomerantz and George Weinberger, Edwin Greenberg and Elaine Gordon, Randy Turtle, Randy Feldman, Linda Nussbaum, and all of the residents, past and present, of Beit T'Shuvah.

Finally, a personal note.

I had no intention of writing this book. I resisted. And resisted. And Rabbi Mark gently prodded. Then pushed a little. We had coffee every week and talked and laughed and argued. And then I realized there was no longer a question about my doing the book. The book had, in fact, already begun.

Thank you, Rabbi Mark, for getting under my skin and for showing me that anything and everything is possible. You are an inspiration.